D0929611

# DE ALFONCE TENNIS

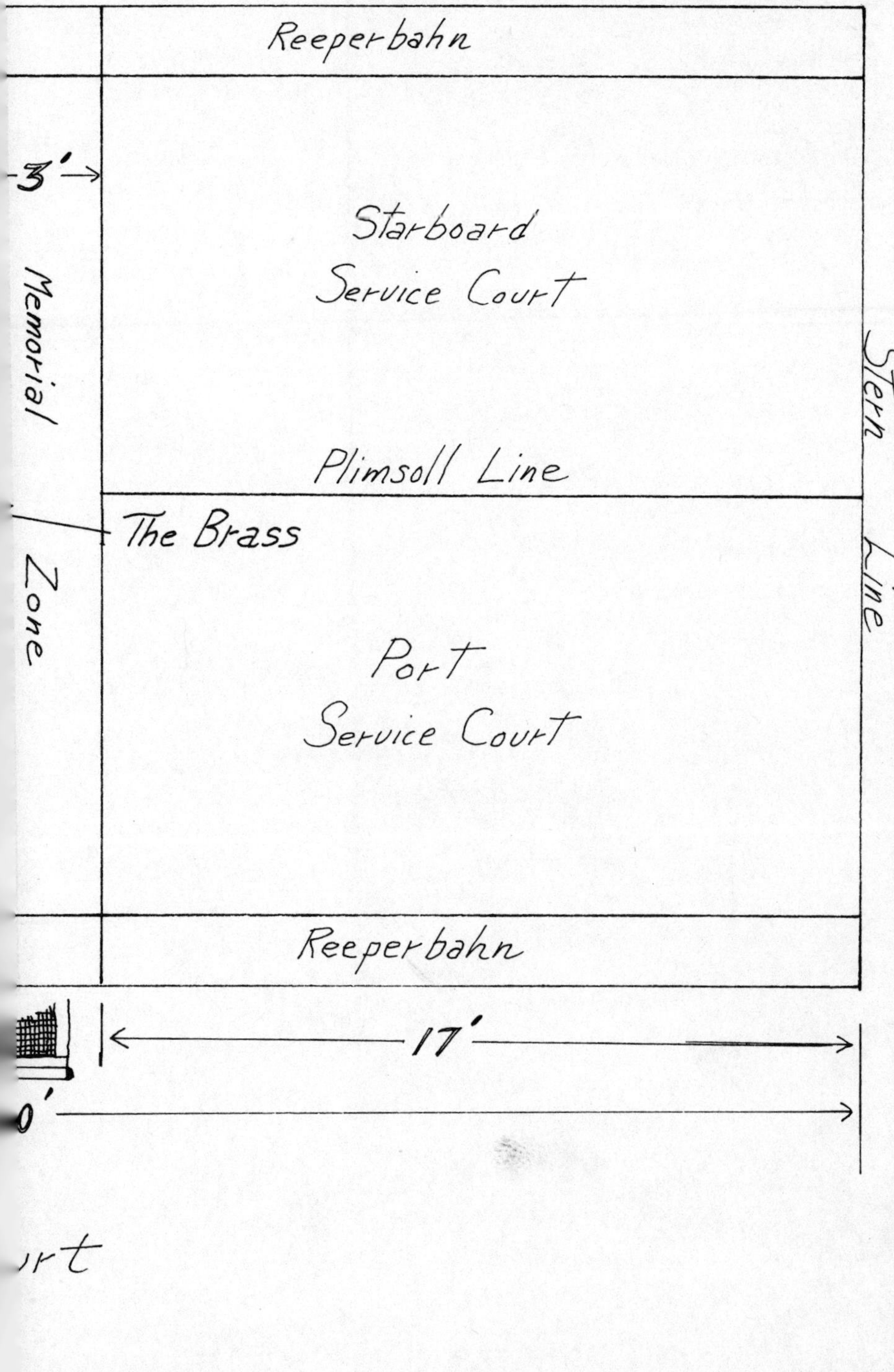

Reeperbahn

Starboard
Service Court

Plimsoll Line

The Brass

Port
Service Court

Reeperbahn

Memorial

Zone

Stern Line

3'

← —————— 17' —————— →

0' —————————————————————→

rt

# J. P. DONLEAVY

# De ALFONCE TENNIS

### THE
### SUPERLATIVE GAME
### OF ECCENTRIC CHAMPIONS
### ITS HISTORY, ACCOUTREMENTS,
### RULES CONDUCT AND
### REGIMEN

WEIDENFELD AND NICOLSON
LONDON

J.P. Donleavy

© 1984 De Alfonce Tennis

The
Superlative Game
of Eccentric Champions
Its History, Accoutrements,
Rules Conduct And
Regimen

ISBN 0 297 785427

Printed in Great Britain by
Butler & Tanner Ltd, Frome and
London

TO
PHILIP DONLEAVY
One of the Eccentrics
and
DE ALFONCE
Singles Champion
of
The Game Club 1983–1984

## Second Dedication

This manual book is also humbly dedicated to the memory of the original coach and oarsmen mentioned herein and to the memory of the lives of those thirteen stalwart physical culturalists presumed lost from the motor yacht 'Hiyathere' without whose sad disappearance the game of De Alfonce Tennis would never have come into being, and to that inimitable gentleman the 'Fourteenth' whose lonely invention and final will and testicle made this sport possible. But most of all to Laura who revealed the first joys of De Alfonce Tennis and made a brief span of my life so idyllic and also so sadly profoundly painful. And least of all to my rival the urinatingly indiscriminate Lord Charles whom finally one grew to not too much detest. Plus to Lieutenant A.K. Alias of the New York Police force, whose grim duties never prevented him from remaining charming, scholarly and wise.

# Contents

ix

CONTENTS

# CONTENTS

CONTENTS

CONTENTS

# CONTENTS

# PREFACE

Upon Squash, Badminton, Lacrosse, Basketball, Handball and even Chess players, among others, who oft times stood in the wings silently watching and then would follow me off court to ask in awe as to what the game was one was playing, and then consequent upon imprecations from its handful of devoted practitioners, I finally was prevailed upon to write the present Manual, in order that this venerable and long nearly secretly played sport could reach out from its small rarefied confines to spread its playing pleasure to the rest of the world.

I had no idea at the time of starting out on this solitary task, that its history when written would prove so mysteriously involved and at times even ominous, or that there would be a gloriously stunning woman, of whom one would helplessly be enamoured, and who would give the game its birth, or that relating it, would take the unearthing of so many files and memorabilia, not to mention haunting enigma. And although it has cost me much in heartache recalling some painful moments in its telling, my hopes are that such tristfulness shall be small penance indeed for the jubilation that I and all other De Alfonce Tennis players enjoy when stepping out to balletically wield our racquets on court once more.

### APOLOGUE

He is a rare man who hasn't many a time
given long moments to disillusionment and
despair but it is the sensible man who, thus
suffering, then seizes his racquet, gets up on
his hind legs, lofts his ball, and upon serving
a sizzling winner, hollers loud and clear to
his opponent standing lax in his tracks, 'Be
damned sir, the mumpish miseries, and let's
say hello to wholesome perspiration.'

ANONYMOUS
*The Game Club Locker Room*
*circa 1938*

If God invented man, he then damn bloody well quickly invented the ball and racquet to amuse him.

Horatio Josiah De Alfonce Adams iv
'The Fourteenth'
*The Game Club Tap Room*
*December 5th 1941*
*7.15 p.m.*

# CAUTION

BEFORE ADOPTING THE ROUTINES, MANNERISMS, DEPORTMENT AND REGIMEN SPELLED OUT UPON THE PAGES OF THIS MANUAL, YOU ARE REQUESTED BEFORE ATTEMPTING ANYTHING IT MAY PROMULGATE, TO FAITHFULLY READ IT COVER TO COVER, THEN UPON HAVING YOUR DOCTOR, BANKER AND SPIRITUAL ADVISER OR FORTUNE TELLER DO LIKEWISE, INSIST THAT THEY ACCORDINGLY EXAMINE YOU PHYSICALLY, FINANCIALLY, MORALLY AND HOROSCOPICALLY, TO DETERMINE YOUR FITNESS TO BECOME A DE ALFONCE PLAYER AND TO CONFORM TO SUCH PURSUIT AS A WAY OF LIFE. HOWEVER, SINCE SUCH ADVISERS ARE MORE THAN OCCASIONALLY WRONG, YOU MAY ALSO HAVE TO DEPEND UPON YOUR OWN SOLE JUDGEMENT, IN WHICH CASE, YOU WILL BE TAKING YOUR FIRST STEP ON YOUR WAY TO BEING ONE OF US.

# HISTORY

## THE GAME

The gentle, dramatically satisfying, quietly astonishing and splendidly spectacular game of De Alfonce Tennis is with these words hereby officially invented and ordained with its name, rules and conduct.

As a sport and art it can be enjoyed by all ages and manner of multidemeanoured humankind not excluding even those slightly less than totally infirm. Tactically skilled and played with its feather light racquet and feather light ball over a net on a small court and indulged at full stretch, it can be as fast as the ability of the players allows. As one accustoms to the soft pneumatics of the ball, a high degree of competence can be immediately achieved. The ball, whose initial velocity gracefully decelerates from the impact of the light swift speed of the racquet, provides that additional extra split second for the body to set itself, which allows for extremely accurate hitting. The execution of spin and slice strokes involving wrist, hand as well as a whip like arm action can administer to the ball a unique control, keeping it in play and permitting the ultimate in the subtleties of disguise. Power and speed alone cannot dominate this sport, but wits, strategy, patience and concentration can. For these and many more reasons has the game been proclaimed superlative.

## ANCIENT HISTORY

Although the first official De Alfonce Tennis Singles and Doubles match played under rules took place during the weekend of the great New York blizzard of February 1983, the game's origins trace back through a series of coincidences and bizarre accidents not to mention mystery, spanning more than fifty years. The first occurring high up in an enormous room of The Game Club, a great soaring variant of an Italian Renaissance palace, which has long been

3

a fabled monument given to the exclusive pursuit of gentlemanly sports.

It was in this grey stone edifice on an extremely beastly inclement day in the late 1930s that an aristocratically disciplined coach of a rowing crew, in order to exercise his charges indoors, suspended a bright crimson ribbon between two chairs over which his oarsmen would hand hit a ball back and forth. As these scrupulously trained gentlemen increasingly became competitive in this activity, the coach distributed specially made doeskin gloves, erected a net in place of the ribbon and drew lines on the floor, finally giving rise to the first and alas, only terra firma based court upon which a game, later eccentrically named Bangkok Boxo Ball, proceeded to be played for the next eleven years.

With its vicious serving tactics and complicated oriental scoring rules, accompanied by bows and alien grunting sounds, Bangokok by which shorter name it became jocularly known, frequently gave rise to loud and occasionally violent fisticuff arguments over line calls and the correct interpretation of its altogether novel rules. As a result, this sport, because of the objections voiced by other member users of the great chamber, became separated from the rest of the room by opaque green drapes made of specially sound deadening material.

Over the ensuing years, despite bloody noses, cracked ribs and the increasingly missing teeth of its socially registered players, the court continued to be used in its cloistered confines, but was now flanked by Art Nouveau satinwood seating benches installed to accommodate peacekeeping referees. This curious pastime however, did attract a certain thrill seeking variety of raccoon fur coated heirs to large American fortunes, whose luxuriously casual afternoons required the antidote of some boisterous amusement. And a handful, referred to as the 'Bangokok Boys' took up the sport with some gusto.

One of these latter gentlemen, fond of perpetrating physi-

cally dangerous pranks after which he would attempt to
mollify his victim with his equally dangerous backslapping,
invited all his fellow Bangokok players for an overnight
Saturday cruise with their lady companions aboard his
yacht. This ocean going 226 foot classed Lloyd's 100 A1
motor ship with its Panama hatted, double breasted raw silk
suited male guests and its twenty nine man crew was, in the
dusk of the pre dinner cocktail hour, sighted in its seafaring
merriment, steaming north east in calm seas opposite Sa-
gaponack, four miles off this dune studded Long Island
shore. The vessel, expected to round Montauk Point and
anchor in Sag Harbor at eleven that evening with tables
booked to dine at the American Hotel, was never to be seen
or heard of again.

Thus in one fell swoop, or dunking, did the game of
Bangokok disappear. Leaving only a memorial wreath that
each year, on the fatal day, used to be placed, until his
demise, on the floor of the court by the fourteenth player
who having had to attend upon the death of his mother did
not make the ill destined voyage. The Chairman of the
Badminton Committee of the Great Room is responsible
for the bronze commemorative plaque, with its anchor symbol flanked by a severed hand and ball, which has been

5

embedded in the floor of the court, mid net, listing the thirteen players' names who had once roared, accused, wrong footed each other, and scowled in the drape enclosed arena where their beloved game was played. Adding to the mystery was the presence on board of the Club Bangokok Singles Champion, an old salt, unbeaten for the last seven straight years, who was openly detested by his host, and also happened to be a famed yachtsman Commodore on active duty in the Coast Guard. Stories that a giant white shark over thirty feet in length had earlier that day, in a frenzy, charged charter boats in the area, were discounted as having anything to do with the peculiar disappearance.

## MODERN HISTORY

This hauntingly strange incident which some thought a host's prank gone wrong, remained unreported at the time due to its uncanny occurrence on the eve of the Japanese attack on Pearl Harbor which brought America's immediate entry into the Second World War. The suppression of the story was thought to relate to the interests of national security but the rumour that the vessel was seized by an enemy power was vigorously denied by the then Secretary of the Navy. Nevertheless it left a pall over the unused Bangokok court which persisted for many years and was not finally lifted till the miracle of exercise hit the new breed of gung ho young executive ascending to his niche among the American mercantile elite and who sought to prevent the bicep softening and buttock flattening caused by attendance at the corporate desk.

But mention of Bangokok still variously surfaced, especially in association with stories, progressively more embroidered, that there had been, in various parts of the world, spottings and sightings of these previous singularly vanished sporting gents. A popular newspaper actually front paging a photograph purporting to be of the legendary yacht owner together with the 'old salt' Commodore, arms about each other's shoulders, drinking in a Munich beer cellar and the picture captioned with the name of the departed vessel, 'Hiyathere'. Other sightings of other Bangokok players and even their ladies, were reputed to have been made in an Austrian coffee house in Salzburg and in seamier haunts such as the Reeperbahn of Hamburg. In recent years the original tragedy and tabloid provoked rumours have for the most part, died down and the memory of those stalwart gentlemen has been obliterated by yet another aggressive generation of vigorous keep fit adherents who have invaded the original Bangokok court in pursuit of their own devised game, a very pedestrian pastime called Sockoball.

This new group consisting of prominent physicians and astonishingly physically tall lawyers clearly welcomed the refreshing leg stretching change from billing clients and scalpel wielding over hot operating tables, and initially took to disappearing behind the green drapes to shout, curse and remonstrate with gusto, punching their hard black rubber sphere back and forth. However the game of Sockoball, without the inviting vigorous eccentricity and hair raising violence of Bangokok, never attracted sufficient players or more probably perhaps, did finally bore its new adherents. And slowly but surely all drifted away to other sports, and the court was left yet again abandoned to its memorial plaque and once a year silent wreaths. That is, until two widely publicized incidents involved the last of the original players of Bangokok who had become known in club circles as the 'Fourteenth'.

This supremely fit and greyingly handsome gentleman, an amateur cryptologist and a collector of rare music boxes, who usually placed a wreath on the court to commemorate the disappearance of his former Bangokok cronies, instead held a bizarre memorial service at a well known Park Avenue Protestant Church. The ceremony at five p.m. on this

Friday the thirteenth included a brief address from the vicar following which Tchaikovsky's 'Capriccio Italien' was played by full orchestra. Present in the small audience was the 'Fourteenth' and his diminutively pretty Japanese girl-friend who were surrounded by thirteen hired masked mimes in white silk suits and Panama hats. The music performed was that heard on the calm evening on the Saga-ponack shore when the strains reached the ears of a musically knowledgeable gentleman taking an evening stroll on the sands.

It was because of this unusual memorial service, that the 'Fourteenth' was to be interviewed live on a midnight national talk show when he was expected to relate his reminiscences as a Bangokok player and discuss the still unsolved mystery of the disappearance of 'Hiyathere'. However the interview was automatically cancelled by a single thirty calibre bullet believed fired from the roof of a building an entire block away and fatally hitting the 'Fourteenth' as he stood with his Pomeranian dog on the top doorstep of an elegant east side town house. His lady friend, described by neighbours as like an exquisite Dresden doll, and from whom information was sought by police, has not been found.

These discomforting events again focused attention on the green draped arena of the Bangokok court. Inspiring a handful of mildly eccentric young Wall Street corporation executives to tie their longer strands of hair back in the manner of the American Indian, and to sport white yachting caps, while attempting to again play this game. But with only a few remaining ancient aged veterans hanging about the Great Room, who refer to themselves as 'us old fogies whom no one gives a good god damn about anymore' the efforts of the 'tie their hair back chaps' to revive the original grunt and snort game of Bangokok failed. And these young executives too, finally gravitated back to Squash, Badminton, and for those fancying kicks on the shins and socks on the jaw, to Soccer and Rugby.

8

Sad though that this was and sad too that the bizarre strangely ritualistic sport of Bangokok has not since been heard mentioned in the Great Room, nor its commemorative floor plaque polished, nor its fourteenth name been there added, nor any further explanation been forthcoming regarding the strangely vanished thirteen, yet that sport, with all its subsequent tantalizing mystery, has unwittingly, from the moment its first fluttering crimson ribbon stretched tight between two chairs, set the scene for the discovery of the elegantly benign, and most astonishing sport of all, De Alfonce Tennis.

## THE INVENTION

The funeral of the 'Fourteenth', which I attended as a long time superficial but always warmly cordial acquaintance, took place from an elegant Madison Avenue undertaker's attracting a large gathering as the 'Fourteenth' was a member of many of New York's elitist clubs, and a passionate botanist. And blossoms were blooming on this unseasonably sultry day, as the bronze casket was interred during a violent thunderstorm drenching many of the mourners who jam packed the large family mausoleum, which also contained many manorial artefacts, including an organ, a replica of that in the Church of St Sulpice in Paris, and upon which Gounod's 'St Cecilia Mass' was played.

The internment was attended by the famed homicide detective, Lieutenant A. K. Alias, under whose jurisdiction the case came for investigation. This scholarly sleuth had for years entirely by coincidence, made a study of the mysterious case of the disappearance of 'Hiyathere'. The Lieutenant, piecing together information that two of the thirteen spoke fluent Japanese and another, although an amateur, was a brilliant atomic physicist as well as the Game Club chess champion, had also discovered that the host, the owner of 'Hiyathere' was a recognized world authority on cryogenics, and all but five of his shipboard guests had been members of a secret society at Yale College given to occult practices. And finally that all were, nearly without exception, bachelors and some of the richest men in America, the Lieutenant commenting 'and with that kind of freedom and financial back up, you can afford to have a few kinks'.

On the day of the funeral, the interviewed Lieutenant said the mystery was still very much alive as a sighting had been verified as recently as six months ago, when the so called and now departed 'Fourteenth' and the Commodore were recognized having dinner together at the Hotel de Paris in Monte Carlo and overheard speaking fluent Russian. The Lieutenant commenting 'so who doesn't act strange once in a while in their lives, but it still doesn't all add up to a conspiracy'.

As this present author was leaving the mausoleum in this renowned Bronx cemetery, and squeezing past several Yale alumni who were standing regarding with appreciation the massive solid bronze door with its foxhunting scenes of 'The Chase' and 'The Kill' in relief, I was whispered to by the 'Fourteenth's' lawyer, who after enquiring of my identity, requested I attend his office at my convenience in reference to the 'Fourteenth's' will which provided for a certain matter regarding me.

The still sultry next morning while taking breakfast of honey, bran muffin and coffee, I read that Lieutenant Alias had overnight revealed to the press, that the 'Fourteenth', since the death of his mother, was the last in his once socially prominent line, and had in fact committed suicide, having hired a professional assassin to fire from an armorially decorated silver cartridge, a diamond tipped bullet. The Lieutenant announcing that further clues might be expected to be revealed when the dust had settled following the reading of the departed gentleman's will, which, 'greed being what it is these days should materialize many phoney claimants concerning the disposition of his considerable assets and priceless music box collection'.

On the eighteenth floor in a corner office looking upwards along Madison Avenue and with the sun beaming in, I was handed a key to unlock a large gleamingly polished leather box resembling a shotgun case. Which lid upon coming open produced the strains of the 'Capriccio Italien' in all its simple muted harp strumming beauty. And set in the brocaded emerald velvet interior were four bright yellow balls and two strange racquets. And facing me inside the case cover, was a brass plate upon which were engraved the following words:

My dear chap, J.P., I hope certain of us are above certain of the worst characteristics attributed to human beings and in this flavour of spirit, and whether I be dead or alive, I present to you the herewith and admonish that there let be continued beneficial civilized and elegant sport on that court from whence my beloved 'guys' have departed. I entrust to you thus, this, in humble tribute to your reassuringly eccentrically comic thoughts with which I was fondly familiar, not to mention mildly obsessed, over the years, and I hereby bequeath, grant and assign to you this case, and all prior art intrinsic in its contents, together with any and all future invention to which they may be put by your fertile mind, and in small token to you for all the guffaws and chuckles your publicly unappreciated, but nonetheless much privately enjoyed scribbles have given me over the years. And now that I think of it, you may as well have too, and I hereby further bequeath and confer the right, the power and authority to you, of invoking my family's ancient curse, the De Alfonce curse, upon any or all those who would wish to deprive you or to do you or yours, ill.

Toodle oo till then and I know you wish me bon voyage.

The Fourteenth

## The Aftermath

For some many months the elegant brass cornered leather case, with its musical and sporting contents bequeathed me by the 'Fourteenth', resided forgotten, wrapped in a towel in my club locker. And it was not until my annual presence in Salzburg to listen to opera and while indulging a mid morning apfelstrudel in the very Austrian coffee house rumoured to have witnessed the presence of a couple of the 'Bangokok Boys', that one was again reminded of the 'Fourteenth' as my eye confronted an item in the European edition of an American newspaper.

### EUNUCHS TOO AND NOW
### STRANGE SHIP BOARD SPORT
### SURFACES IN SUICIDE MURDER

Another new twist has been revealed in the unsolved murder suicide of the socially prominent polo playing Horatio Josiah De Alfonce Adams IV of New York, who was the odd man out survivor many years ago, in the never explained disappearance off Long Island, of the palatial yacht 'Hiyathere'.

Lieutenant Alias of the New York City Police Department who regards this as one of his most baffling cases, told this reporter that from a copy of the boat's building plans and design, that the vessel, constructed in a Dutch shipbuilding yard, secretly contained just aft of amidships, an air conditioned room sixty feet long, thirty feet wide and two decks deep which housed a court for Bangokok, an eccentric game exclusively played by all the gentlemen on board who disappeared with their lady friends and ship's crew on the voyage.

Of particular note on the ship was an engineering phenomenon, the court's ceiling, a solid sheet of glass which not only was used in play, but spanning the entire court, allowed spectators in the ship's salon to view the game from above. The luxurious motor yacht had specially constructed stabilizers installed in the hull, unique at the time, to keep the ship steady during a match in progress.

Although Lieutenant Alias is interested in pursuing the part that Bangokok played in the murder victim's life including the curious coincidence of the 'Fourteenth's' fluent Russian and German speaking Japanese girlfriend and the implications that this posed with the 'Hiyathere' disappearing on the eve of the Japanese attack on Pearl Harbor, he would not speculate as to whether this had any wartime political implications, but he did say that the 'Fourteenth' had prior to the final voyage, long been an outspoken Bangokok dissident, and had been devising a new ball and a racquet to be used on shipboard as well as on the original terra firma court.

As to the other mysteries associated with the original tragedy, the Lieutenant said he has recently given more credence to the oft repeated rumour that the vanished all male crew of the 'Hiyathere' were shanghaied, castrated and converted into eunuchs. Nor does he totally discount the story that the ladies aboard were abducted into white slavery. As the Lieutenant was rushing off to another homicide he ad libbed over his departing shoulder 'I don't know how the eunuchs are liking their role but the ladies may not have suffered such a bad fate, some of those harems are a lot fancier than our best split level sylvan suburban homes.'

During further stunned rereadings of the article I not only had another coffee but also popped back a much impromptu large brandy as well. Exactly two months later I was travelling by ocean liner to the United States and cutting short one's further European lonely lurkings in Paris and Amsterdam to attend a litigation in progress in New York. And one stormy mid Atlantic evening while about to ladle up my last taste of Vichyssoise at the Captain's table, to which I was invited by my new dinner partner, a most elegantly agreeable young lady, I was requested to the bridge 'radio shack' for an urgent telephone call.

With the raging storm, the signals' officer had me come there as he was having great difficulty in tuning to a hearable frequency and in the long delay graciously had my savoury glazed fillets of Dover Sole Waleska summoned along from the dining room. And in the middle of a mouthful I nearly choked. For troubling me this evening during the hors d'oeuvres was the identity of a diner sitting with his exquisite female oriental companion. Now suddenly his strangely familiar face dawned on me, as being none other than the former Bangokok player, the famed yachtsman Commodore of the Coast Guard. And just as a helpful radio man wiped the sauce stain from my dinner jacket and trousers, I nearly gagged once more as the very next moment the voice crackling in my ear over the windswept north Atlantic, was that of Lieutenant Alias.

With the storm worsening, I held on in the ponderous pitching and rolling of the ship, straining to hear through the static and shrieks of the gale roaring outside. And I tried to bellow my news of the sighting to the Lieutenant, but his own shouting voice drowned out mine, finally making himself understood only enough to communicate that he wished to interview the present owner of the case containing the 'Fourteenth's' invented racquet and ball, and he understood I was that person.

Upon returning to the dining room for one's waiting Boned Breast of Guinea Hen with Ham Lucullus, the Bangokok Commodore and his companion were gone. Nor did he reappear for the remainder of the voyage. As I was strenuously trying to work off such things as Cornets of Smoked Salmon and Beluga Caviare, plus Flambé Pêches in Kirschwasser and selected Petits Fours, I accepted the invitation of my lady dinner partner to play long bouts of squash each

NEW MOON FLOWER
Rare Specimen
Collected by the 'Fourteenth'

afternoon. She, even in her purposeful athletic gear, was an appetizingly curvacious classically beautiful raven haired variety of an English rose who conveniently was also an awfully large shareholder in the present steamship line, and to whose inquisitive explorations the entire ship seemed to be open. And I followed her private excursions through engine rooms, chain lockers, kitchens and even the medicinal baths, in each of which she would invariably remark, 'Don't you find all these inner sanctums awfully excitingly educational.'

Not only could this irrepressibly amusing lady devastate me at squash but her unquenchable curiosity and questions and my somewhat embroidered answers, fanned the mystery of 'Hiyathere' into nearly nightmarish proportions. Her marvellously strong fast legs would suddenly plant themselves, and with her awesomely female posterior stiffening slightly she would throw her coccyx forward, and remark, 'Surely J.P. you must track down, and get the ship's doctor to examine, to see if that Commodore Coast Guard person you think you recognize, is still possessed of his manly attributes. Certainly his oriental companion simply reeks of the ill gotten gains from white slavery.'

Laura, as she was called, also took a proprietary interest in the contentment of every elderly, ignored and lonely third class passenger, dragging me by the hand, to descend into the ship's lower regions where she would spend long sessions talking or playing draughts with them. But her attentions too could also turn in the direction of the various first class sun deck portholes whose curtains might be parted as we passed. And peering into one she jumped back, covering her eyes, 'O dear me, something I fear one was not perhaps meant to see.' Taxed as to the nature of her eyeballful, she giggled, jumping her eyebrows up and down, saying, 'And wouldn't you like to know and solve your whole "Hiyathere" mystery.'

Laura continued to tease me through squash, leaving me sweatingly defeated in three games, and then in the verandah lounge, having spattered my tie with Devon cream, succeeded in pouring hot tea over my knee. Until finally on her way again to the poor needy passengers in tourist class, I suggested she wanted to slum a bit before dinner. And we had a wrestling match as I tried to control her arms from slapping me. And under the duress of my arm twisting, she pretended to divulge that she had seen the oriental lady in awfully sparse costume performing an erotic dance, not only in front of the possibly neutered Commodore, but also the French professor. The latter being one of her favourite passengers who sat in white tie and tails solitarily dining nearby in view of the Captain's table and whose habit it was, arriving at meals, to turn towards us before he sat down, and bow to the stunning ladies there, one by one, and especially to Laura, who would purringly remark 'O what a very sweet gentleman he is to make us poor ladies feel so esteemed.'

Of course I apologized for casting aspersions upon her motives among the third class passengers. And she craned her head teasingly forward to whisper. 'And now my dear J.P. wouldn't you like to know what they were really doing instead of what I previously have totally fabricated.' Then she ran laughing down the companionway, chased by me, to nip into a ladies' convenience and therein shout out an invitation to enter and get her. I was now imagining that I was on some kind of nutty spy ship. And even that Laura, who declared herself a Buddhist who would never kill any living thing, might really be a devastatingly effective undercover agent of the British Secret Service. For, to all my questions as to why she was going to America, she invariably answered with her bright blue eyes sparkling above her dazzling grin, 'And wouldn't you like to know.'

Being on the verge of being between wives at the time, I naturally became quite undone by Laura and more than mildly jealous when I saw her smile at another. And she was, as I suspected, a former squash champion. Her father a bishop and her mother owning an eccentric Victorian pile, one of Britain's famed stately homes. Where of course one might have known, they had two squash courts. Then hearing of her lone travels through Africa and Kashmir she became an even greater enigma. Having lived in Katmandu and among the Sherpas and monks of Tibet, she also spoke fluent Sherpa and Nepalese. And had the distinction of being the one female ever permitted to study Buddhist sacred books.

Each morning I woke scanning my copy of the ship's newspaper 'Ocean Times' looking for a topic of conversation in which to engage her as early as I could on the telephone. And delightedly I had happened upon a discreet headline and text.

'INTERMINGLING'
Passengers are kindly requested
to remain in the accommodation
in which they have booked.

Upon Laura hearing it, she gurgled laughing and said, 'You would, wouldn't you like to know who I've got here in my suite with me.' I did not enquire but I noted at her words that my spirits slumped a few decks down in my soul. As one came to expect, her extremely prankish nature produced more and more foolish answers to my more and more inane questions and she always giggled at me in the same vein, 'My dear J.P. of course in Tibet I was trying to meet the abominable snowman and also, being among so many men who have renounced marriage, naturally one attempted to break all those nice little short haired monks of their terribly dull vows of chastity.' If sufficient shock did not register on my face, she always had an aside to add, 'And of course J.P., on the opportune occasions I always strolled about in the nude. And when I have a mind to, I can be extremely nude.'

Aside from Laura's excursions down to steerage, this was one of those pleasantly undemocratic voyages where the first class mariners strictly kept to themselves. And the passenger list had visibly invisible neon blinking gold stars next to any passenger's name not already graced as an Ambassador or peer of some realm. As one soon heard everyone's occupation and pedigree bandied about, it was hardly necessary, as a social climber, to resort to the ship's library for Debrett or the well thumbed 'Who's Who In The Universe'. Each day the parvenus aboard braved the unsubtle snobbery of worldly wealth and rank as well as the haute cuisine in gale force winds in the hope that an invitation might befall them to an exclusive private party with which the ship was enchantingly alive. And from which the blatantly ambitious were ruthlessly relegated. And of all these jollifications the most elegant but least private was given by Laura.

'Of course J.P. I can't absolutely promise you'll be the absolute centre of attention, but I should be crushed if you did not come.'

On that particular evening I carefully attended to my cuffs and creases. With the storm now behind us, I strolled the deck under a star sprinkled sky. There was a light breeze, rippled sea, and moderate swell. At the stern end of the boat deck I paused to stare out over the rails and suddenly saw a large fin flash across the ship's light on the water. With a sense of the ominous I arrived at Laura's soiree. My black tie retied in the 'gents' so that it did not look, as Laura called it, 'like a crashed aeroplane propeller'. Her suite M70 was thronged, and quite unbelievably commodious. With three bathrooms, large double and one single bedroom plus a sitting and dining room decorated in eau de nil, and trunk space big enough for a family of the leaner sort of tourist class passenger to comfortably travel in. She wore a shimmering magenta gown, her hair so gleamingly black on her white shoulders. And an emerald and diamond necklace, its five ropes suspended above Laura's satiny bosoms, had all the bejewelled dowagers hiding their own paltry gems in shame.

As you might imagine the Captain, Chief Engineer, Surgeon, along with the ship's whole gang of known social top notchers were animatedly assembled. However, true to form, Laura also had her collection of elderly lonely shunned third class passengers. The group of them conducted upwards to her suite by the tourist class purser through the half or so mile of intricate passageways and first class barriers. Which was not altogether applauded by certain of those paying first class fare.

Laura could only spare me a wave and grin between the heads, several of whom in awe were regarding Laura's collection of Impressionist paintings on the walls. I was pronto crushed by a pushy person up against a tallboy and asked 'Excuse me are you someone important whose name

I should know, and ha ha, who is worth knowing.' And as one does at such times one wondered why one had ever been singled out for Laura's regard in the first place. I did think in my more optimistic moments that I was at least facially free of the worst of my peasantly ethnic character-istics and presentable enough to deserve at least her occa-sional acknowledgement if not her attentions. But upon dis-covering why she had me invited to the Captain's table, I was totally dashed to learn it was because, 'You looked so sadly out of it all.' She evidently had noticed the first day at sea that I was in the main lounge tucked in a corner behind the grand piano, simply sitting alone talking to no one, and staring into space. She said, 'In your terribly for-bidding Victorian clothes and that tie you wear, I thought at the most optimistic prospect you might be a funeral di-rector. Then when I saw you occupying such an anonymous table way over by the entrance to the kitchens, and again all by yourself, and clearly so desperately needing mother-ing, I just felt something had to be done. Loneliness is, don't you think, the most dire of all pain.'

Nor was Laura as she said, travelling alone. Occupying her suite with her was an extremely well built but faintly masculine young lady always in a rather drab military green dress, who seemed only to appear mornings and afternoons, either strolling the boat deck or occupying a lonely deck-chair outside the dog kennels, where her massive Irish wolfhound had his accommodation. And on the tallboy against which I was being crushed was a picture, among several other silver framed photographs, of them both standing in whites with racquets on a Royal Tennis Court. Then, just as I was about to turn away to ease out of my entrapment, my eye caught another photograph behind the rest. Laura, clearly some years younger, and again on a Royal Tennis Court, posed centre of the gently sloping net, coronets studded in the background, and in the spine chill-ing company of none other than the 'Fourteenth'.

As one who was currently unpleasantly involved in litigation, I was extremely hesitant to broach the subject of this strange connection to Laura. Plus I certainly began to think I was being followed. And on my next nightly pre dinner excursions on a deserted boat deck, some instinct made me look back over my shoulder, just as a figure shrunk back under a ship's lifeboat. And when I turned and confronted the face of this young blond aristocrat he said yes. 'As a matter of fact I am following you, I want to know why such an unprepossessing type like you with no discernible distinctions, should attract the most beautiful woman aboard this ship, you bastard you.' The tone he used in uttering the word bastard nearly made me strike him on the spot, but I could see it was exactly what the inebriated fellow wanted. Instead, as I had been an undergraduate at a very English university, I availed of an appropriate response. 'You little awful twit you.'

I soon discovered from my other table partner, a British Ambassador's wife, that this little awful twit was the younger son of a Marquis being shipped off by his fed up family to acquaint with the harsh facts of life on a ranch way up a dry gulch in Nevada. And that he was conspicuously lovesick over Laura, following her everywhere he could, and upon being even the slightest bit ignored by her, would then drunkenly threaten to jump overboard. He even sneaked his way to lie in wait on the balcony to watch us play squash. The little bastard applauding every point she won. Nightly he would, when drunk enough, maraud among the dance orchestra and urinate off the dais. Once putting his foot and then his head through a drum. Until finally I heard a commotion going by my stateroom door, and a sorely tried sergeant at arms telling him that he would be clapped in irons and put below. To which the young Lord proclaimed loudly 'Get your fucking commoner cocksucking hands off me or you'll be damn sorry.'

Certainly I found the young Lord's fighting spirit impressive but did not relish his insulting presence next day when I was calling by Laura's suite to play squash. I was left twenty minutes in her sitting room while she attempted to shoo him away from her door. And while waiting I noticed an elaborately embellished small ivory casket, the cover of which one could not help lifting. Inside were the elaborate bejewelled workings of a music box playing part of a singularly sad obscure Opus by Janáček and inside the lid a brass plate engraved with the inscription:

> To my beloved Laura
> A little girl
> Whose beauty
> And spirit
> Shall always play
> In my heart
> As does the music within
> This box
>
> Your ancient admirer
> FONCY

Laura beamed pleasure when I knew the piece of music. Indeed I had often, listening to it, replenished my own spirits with a warmth of hope. And there were tears welling in Laura's eyes as she said, 'A present, J.P., from a dear cousin, I take it with me wherever I go. 'Foncy' was a name I called him, my variation of De Alfonce, being one barrel of his rather considerably barrelled up name.'

It was then at that very moment when the young Lord's voice was again heard out in the companionway plaintively repeating. 'But I love and adore you Laura, don't you understand that. I want to marry you.' And Laura quietly closing her sitting room door, the young Lord's voice no longer heard. Yet most wretched and embarrassing of all was the fact of this young man's words nearly being identical to the very ones I was now oft repeating. But they were spoken down so deep in my soul, that they might never make the long journey to my lips.

'I do worship you Laura and I know you've got that damn commoner in there with you.'

There was another brief commotion out in the companionway. Then silence. I continued to sit in my whites as Laura, her splendid legs emerging from hers, went to speak to Clare in her bedroom. From the arm rest of a chair I took and opened a seemingly torrid romantic novel Laura had been reading, and riffled through the pages, and there, as a marker, was a sheet of paper, one of the ship's daily quizzes, and this one called 'Who?' and which from the handwriting and answers I saw, I realized I had filled out. To questions like who invented dynamite, I mentioned Al Capone and as to who inspired the Suffragette movement in Britain I had supplied a currently well known female impersonator and transvestite, with my entry signed Dr Crippen. And Laura back in the room, blushed crimson, admitting she had picked it up after I'd left my lonely seat that day where she'd first seen me in the main lounge. 'J.P. it did make me laugh and I must confess, it was half why I had the Captain invite you to our table. But the other half reason is not for you to know.'

One is not easily given to vanity, but a tiny glow of self esteem did wend its way upwards from my toe tips into the increasing number of my grey hair ends. But just in case I was being cast in some grotesque conspiracy, having, even at the best of times, a strong tendency to paranoia, I said nothing nor questioned Laura further about the 'Fourteenth' or again mentioned the 'Hiyathere'. Even so, in no event could I ever imagine Laura, who held the lonely and shunned in such kindly concern, to conspire in anything the least untoward. But I was not prepared for the very next very mystifying event at dawn the following morning while we were still a whole day and a half's steaming from New York.

I'd again got a two or three a.m. phone call from Laura, 'Wake up and start living you old grumpy grouch', and begging me come 'save her' from the dance floor, and even to come in my pyjamas. And it had happened, following her previous phone calls, that she had come down to my stateroom. Giving the young Lord the slip as she sped from the promenade down two decks to nip in and hide in the purser's reception room, then taking the waiting lift down to B deck to gently knock at my cabin door.

With my light out, and with such a sweet smelling strangely affectionate lady, one could hardly tell dream from reality. And the contentment one felt, just to be enveloped in her arms, even though in the process, we'd both knocked off our vaccination scabs. And then the consternation. To have the young Lord drunkenly hammering on my state-room door. Challenging me to come out and fight and that 'And if you ever try to sleep with Laura, I'll kill you, you bloody commoner, so help me god, I'll kill you.' And when the other passengers asleep on B deck awakened and sum-moned the sergeant at arms, we were treated to another recital of imperially proclaimed foul language, punctuated with kicks thumps and bumps fading down the companion-way.

Laura who was clearly something only the spiritually minded Tibetans could have invented, made her departure discreetly prior to dawn. She untwined my arms saying, 'Please you have to let me go as I must hurry to answer a call of nature.' I suggested that my own not unsumptuous and fully operative bathroom might do. But Laura de-murred and looking to see if the companionway was clear, quietly closed my door and silently stole away. I lay long awake thinking, as usual about money. How much of it I had left and how much of it I was hopeful of getting. And how soon. As it is never cheap to employ fourteen lawyers as I was currently doing. But if such thoughts in daylight hours had kept me lonely staring out into space, I was grateful for any little good it may have done to attract Laura. Whose recent presence had me now electrically awake thinking of her.

Then a sudden glow of light flashed in my porthole and over my ceiling. And there was an unfamiliar thumping and clanking sound. Having been a former naval person, all shipboard activity especially the exercise of seamanship, took my interest. I noticed the liner's movement had noticibly slowed and then seemed with a brief reverse of engines, to be still in the water. I got out of bed to look out my stateroom porthole. And just abeam in the grey lifting mist, a couple of cable lengths away, a naval frigate was hove to flying an admiral's flag. Having earlier on the trip requested my steward to loosen the porthole screw bolts, I was just able to half stick my head to crane an eye to see that a stair gangway down the ship's side was being taken up, and at the same moment I could feel we were under way again. And high up along the ship's rail I saw the unmistakable bejewelled arm of Laura sticking out from the black wall of the riveted hull and waving down to a small tender cutting through the low swell upon which I could only discern figures and shapes. But standing in the tender's cockpit and about to enter its cabin, two of these shapes were also unmistakable. One was that of the diminutive oriental lady and the other the short powerfully built figure of the 'Bangokok' Commodore.

The 'Ocean Times' and a general knowledge quiz usually shoved under my door were instead on my tray as my steward arrived with a late breakfast. Alongside my toast was a folder 'Landing Arrangements' with a dictionary of instructions. Weather and other circumstances permitting we were expected to dock at 2.30 p.m. next day. One day late due to reduced speed earlier in the journey during the two day storm. These last moments my steward was dancing

extra special attendance upon one. With a jolly gung ho
tone to his voice. 'Are we shipshape this morning sir.
Rather rough sea, strong south westerly breeze and moderate heavy swell. Also I fear we are rather overcast.' Then
he reached down. 'Dear me sir, we don't want to step on
this.' My steward handed me a necklace from the floor. Of
five strings of petit pois sized diamonds, the centre string
studded with eight acorn sized emeralds and a ninth the
size of a modest chestnut. It was nearly eleven o'clock. And
a moment after the steward left, there was a most god awful
pounding on my door.

'I am demanding entry sir and to search your cabin. Open
up.'

Before my teeth could release from one of a compote of
pears and speak, the little pipsqueak Lord was already in
my door, confronting me. Clearly he was taking a holiday
from his daily caterwauling outside Laura's suite. Although
an ungainly six foot or more he was fast on his feet. And
had already taken a further giant step in my direction.

'You are sir as well as being a damn imposter and cad,
also clearly a low down thief.'

There was of course on the blond satinwood of my bedside table, conspicuously next to the ivory coloured telephone, the necklace. And one had no inkling of chance to
deny any knowledge of such a bauble to this damn nuisance,
or to meanwhile somehow make its safe return to Laura.
One knew not much but enough about jewellery to know
this singular piece was not paste and alone could pay my
fourteen lawyers sufficient for them to all retire to Monaco.

'I say, by jove you've just been sizing up its value haven't
you.'

Amazingly fast, the young aristo pounced like a tiger. My
elbow smeared my velvety portion of truffled foie gras as I
upended my bedroom tray, trying to pull myself out from
under the bedcovers. Knocking over a pitcher of thick
cream, and spilling the contents of my coffee pot over my-

self. The little twit Lord already having the necklace in his
fist. I grabbed the lapels of his jacket. And as he wrenched
away I dug my hand over his collar and tore it open. Shud-
dering to see exposed on his neck, scars of a rope. Flowers
sent by Laura were toppled in their vase to the floor soaking
the carpet. My toes could feel my delicious black grapes
being fatally trampled as one kicked around oranges and
apples from my previously peacefully poised fruit bowl. A
blinding flash of pain seemed to explode in my left eye and
another on my nose which latter was now copiously cascad-
ing blood.

'You spivvy commoner bastard crook also engaged in
communist sleazy espionage.'

The tall slender Lord about whose previously strangled
neck I was now compressing my fingers, turned out to be
unbelievably strong. I held on as he crashed me back
against my writing desk. The son of a bitch once out of my
cabin would be proclaiming his accusation all over the ship.
To make me a highly unpleasing person to other first class
passengers during the remainder of the journey. Not to
mention being arrested on disembarking. Especially as it
could easily be proven I needed the money. I now realized
why it obviously took three and sometimes four members
of the crew to put him to bed at night.

'Why you disgusting cowardly proletarian, in your
scruffy cabin trying to choke me.'

As he still clutched the necklace I at least had the advantage of two hands to his one. But again and again, as we
now tumbled all over the wretched cabin, making an un-
appetizing fruit salad on my carpet, he managed to let land
another contusion somewhere on my head. The son of a
bitch now convinced I was really some sort of con man spy
preying on rich passengers. Of course now too, I was put
in the position of not compromising the reputation of
Laura. That if I didn't steal her necklace, it might have
then been left behind by her in my stateroom.

'I knew all along you were a filthy con man. As if you didn't know Laura has inherited one of the largest fortunes in America. Communist cad.'

The bedtable was knocked over. And who wouldn't, even as a temporarily impoverished capitalist have communist sympathies at a time like this, as he crashed me into the wardrobe door and left it half hanging from a hinge. I shoved him as hard as I could hoping to topple him backwards over my chair. And succeeded. But I went with him. There was a dull clunk as the young Lord's head cracked into the bulkhead panelling, and he lay if not dead, then very unconscious. Leaving me distinctly in a nice little bloody kettle of ocean fish. Taking the necklace from his fist, I threw a cold glass of water on his face. Thanking god that he came to. His eyes darting about and ready to get up again into the attack. But as I stood over him, my pyjamas blood smeared and half ripped off, and the edge of my squash racquet aimed down at his skull, he at least seemed to hesitate.

'Go ahead you commie coward crook, hit me with that squash racquet. And then I'm going to break it in two over your head.'

Several diamonds and two emeralds were loose on the floor. The Lord now scrambling to pick them up. Giving me a moment to contemplate not only getting a more lethal defence weapon to hand, but also to wipe the unpleasantly congealing blood from my lips and nose, and to stick my tongue to test the root foundations of two or three teeth distinctly loose in my mouth. However the twit Lord was, with foie gras stuck on his nose, now slowly getting back on his haunches. And one felt the diplomat in one, struggle to put the situation into a more urbane light.

'Here for god's sake is the necklace, which you may return to Laura. Now if you are any sort of gentleman to which it would appear you boast some claim, you'll be sporting enough to realize that even the best people occasionally may be forced by life's problems to stoop momentarily low. The only reason why I took Laura's necklace, was because eighteen of my best thoroughbreds were killed in a fire on my estate in Ireland, and I am rather desperately at this exact moment hard up. I had every intention of repatriating the necklace to her, once I had temporarily used it for collateral in New York for a loan.'

'Why you dirty filthy preposterous liar you, to make up an unbelievable story like that and then tell it to one whose family is distinguished in racing circles for generations. You are so damn pathetic, you're not even worth reporting to the Captain.'

I must confess in the moments that it took to turn our conflict into one of a more rational nature, that I was aided in doing so by my holding, instead of my squash racquet, a sabre. The tip of which was pointed downwards at the scar across the young Lord's throat. The blade polished and sharp was clearly capable of parting his prominent adam's apple into two distinct halves. But it was fast dawning in his young Lordship's skull that were he to return the necklace, without my being branded the thief, that he then might be accused of stealing it.

'You think you're so damn clever don't you, that I would fall for such a stupid story and ruse as that.'

'Then my dear chap, twit, and pipsqueak, the only thing to do is to return it together, with an appropriate story. That we chanced upon the culprit, an errant very third class passenger. Who fought us and thus it will explain my injuries. It will my dear chap help you find some favour with her.'

'I suppose I've got to admit, as a criminal you're jolly damn clever, aren't you. And you're after Laura's money aren't you. And you know she's damn well rich already don't you. Well from now on, you'd better just damn well know, she's got a protector.'

I held my sabre as I went to the bath and rang for the

steward. As I came back the Lord was rising to his feet, his hand smoothing back his blond locks and he was stealing a look at my New York address written on my luggage.

'How the bloody hell did someone like you ever become a member of such a good club. To which, as a member of my London club, it so happens I enjoy reciprocal privileges.'

The Lord's eye was now rapidly moving about my cabin and noticing a photograph on the back of a book I had once scribbled. Not an awfully good book nor a particularly good photograph but at least the latter was of me standing attired in plus twos, on parkland in front of an ancient and rather substantial castle and with a gentleman's thistle cutter resting on my shoulder.

'Sorry I had to pop you one in the eye and nose like that but if you don't mind my asking, is that a picture of where you live.'

'I'm sorry, but I'm afraid I do mind your asking since I think you have already impugned my character enough without also now enquiring into the further and better particulars of my personal and private life.'

The castle the Lord enquired concerning in fact belonged to another Lord, eccentric to the nth degree but nevertheless an old dear friend. But I wasn't disposed to changing the young Lord's impression he already clearly had, that it was mine. Especially as the distraction just managed to allow me to grab up from under the bedclothes Laura's exquisitely embroidered silken pink brassière. In the bath I dressed in my squash whites and could see he was tempted to remark on my long trousers but thought the better of it. He even held the door open as I left my stateroom. And before we reached Laura's suite, he was using my Christian name, and even pumping me for other names of possible contacts he might make in New York. It appeared he had only brought with him his dinner jacket, his present awfully rumpled suit, and twenty pounds sterling. However, entrusted with the Purser, was a lock of Napoleon Bonaparte's hair to sell to the highest bidder, as well as the coat Bonaparte wore at the battle of Waterloo. It was an astonishingly blatant transformation. Making me feel suddenly that it was I who was in the company of a fortune hunting, spying twit of a rogue who was also bogusly flaunting entitlements.

On the way to Laura's suite Lord Charles as I now discovered he was called, was every step, becoming quite increasingly familiar with me and suddenly steered us into the midship's bar, a place which looked a rather too sickly green, rust and yellow at that time of the morning for consuming a bottle of champagne which Lord Charles ordered to be put on my bill. We sat in a curtained corner drinking as he expounded his whys, whereas and what fors.

'Sorry I seemed rather to have knocked you about a bit. You see I happened to have had a tutor who instructed me in boxing. And I am rather adept.'

'I see.'

'Of course I may end up a cowboy but I'm on my way to make a fortune in the new world among all you ghastly vulgar nouveaux. But certainly not to become a type like you who has obviously had to grub about to make money, whereas I am one who was simply born to have such. I've been taught to only take what is beautiful and true seriously. But then one is forced upon occasion to mingle with those with the wrong accents, wrong tailors, and who have been at the wrong schools. But I suppose someone like you happened to be lucky enough to have been sent to Europe to be educated and therefore have succeeded in obscuring some of the worst characteristics of your origins. And I'll be the first to admit you seem to have had some of your American worst edges rubbed off.'

'Thank you.'

'But I'll be damned if I'll compromise my background, and what I stand for just to make an awful lot of money. Of course I don't claim to be an exceptionably lovable person. I daresay one cannot be more laconic than that.'

'No one can't, can one.'

'Of course the true signs of a gentleman are that he should be effortless in his gaiety, unruffled in games, implacably agreeable at meals and supremely at ease at all other times and to regard all other matters in life as expendable. And forgive me if I point out that those are simply too awfully off white sports trousers you are wearing in which to play squash. But you at least must have something to recommend you for a girl like Laura to find you even vaguely interesting. Of course you know don't you she practically owns this bloody awful steamship line.'

'No in fact I didn't know.'

His Lordship threw back a lock of his blond hair and disdainfully sniffed his nose in his cigar smoke as if I were blatantly lying, which of course I was, but he thought the better of taxing me with the matter since now suspecting me of living in a castle, where previous to this knowledge he clearly wouldn't have invited me to a commoner's cat's funeral.

'Well she does. And I mean to say one should marry an exquisitely beautiful lady like Laura who is not destined to end up as a sour old grumpy battle axe when she gets on in years.'

'I think you may have just said the first and only thing I entirely agree with.'

Finishing our champagne we proceeded to Laura's suite where she kissed us both on the cheek and additionally hugged me close a moment to comfort me for my reddened and slowly blackening eyes. She then awfully nonchalantly popped her returned necklace and loose gems back into her alligator skin jewellery box which was then being removed by the Purser to the safe deposit on A deck to join Lord Charles's sartorial remnants of Bonaparte. And it did put the Lord in some favour with her, upon which the unbelievably conceited son of a bitch twit instantly presumed.

'You don't, do you, Laura, my dear, mind awfully if I just make myself comfortable here for a bit.'

When we'd finished playing squash, missing lunch, and down in the deep bowels of the ship, taking a saltwater swim and massage and at Laura's usual insistence, also sampling the Laconicum, Calidarium, Tepidarum and vapour, not to mention the Frigidarium, we were now back desperately peckish outside her suite for afternoon tea. As one stood opening the door, assailed by the perfumes of the beauty salon across the companionway, one paused further at a raised voice and loud music inside.

'I am an imperialist thrown among commoners and I want Laura to be my bride, and for you Clare to be best girl. And I may even ask that social climbing imposter espionage agent to be best man.'

Ensconced in Laura's sitting room sofa, bare feet propped up on the table, reading her magazines, her gramophone blaring, was Lord Charles. On his third bottle of champagne, drunk as a skunk, and wearing one of Laura's Ascot bonnets. He appeared to have been making awfully familiar with the shy lady Clare, who standing in the doorway of the dining room and by her flushed looks, seemed to have already run a marathon around these state rooms. Soon confirmed by the buttons of Lord Charles's fly being wide open.

'Damn the pair of you taking so long. We're drinking a toast here to the American Indian from whom that great continent was so blatantly stolen. And that shall be my first act in the new world to proclaim such injustice befallen the Apache, Navaho, Comanche not to mention the Mohawk, Seneca and Sioux.'

At tea the ganglingly tall little son of bitch devouring the lemon curd and nearly all the scones, then ladling on gobbets of strawberry and gooseberry jam. Then between a mouthful to suddenly point an accusing finger at me just as I was timorously helping myself to the little bit of gooseberry left.

33

'That man Laura has strange visas and stamps in his passport for travel all over Soviet Socialist Republics and its satellite states. Not only is he bloody well undesirably Irish but he also could treacherously be an espionage agent.'

'O dear, certainly J.P. you're not a naughty naughty international intriguer. And is it one's duty I wonder to inform the Captain. Surely Charles masquerading in my bonnet you are aren't you, also painting with a rather full brush.'

'Bloody hell Laura why don't you ask him. The imposter, whose social superior I distinctly am. And Laura why don't you have me invited to the Captain's table.'

'Precisely for the very reason implicit in the remarks you've just made.'

Although Lord Charles's social assertion concerning me was absolutely accurate his allusion to my being an undercover agent was totally preposterous. I had personally no idea of espionage or even a remote interest in spying. Admittedly I did however, as a consequence of several not entirely unamusing extracts from my work over the years finding publication in the Moscow Literary Gazette, experience a little of elevated social life in the company of some of the high and mighty behind the Iron Curtain. But not knowing I was even invited until being secretly escorted there from Budapest where I had innocently gone one autumn to sample the medicinal waters and mud baths. A tall dark devastatingly attractive translator showed up at the Gellért Hotel one morning and with a pair of unbelievably intrepid gastronomes, one a major and the other a colonel in the KGB I was whisked on a pleasure tour of the city and taken that evening to a country château to dine. It was hard to resist the beer, the dumplings, the lady, the music and a curtained private compartment on the plane to Moscow. Where it appeared my sole role was to shoot the shit concerning the more unobvious of behavioural and cultural conflicts of East and West and knock back more than an

Sample visa to which the suspicious
Lord Charles alluded

obvious dram or two of elixir beneath the chandeliers of the inner sanctums of the Kremlin.

'Laura this chap is a cloak and dagger man and should be kept under suspicion. Why should he get a radio phone call. And there is a Russian newspaper and phrase book in his cabin.'

'Do please stop being such a baby and shut up Charles.'

Of course one might have known this pompously aristocratic little twit would be ferreting about in my personal effects as I dressed. The fact of the matter was, that a defecting British traitor, who elevated high in the Kremlin hierarchy, maintained, I am sure erroneously, that I had an unpublic but widespread underground influence on the youth of the upcoming generation and in particular on a handful of those gaining significant positions of power in one or two governments of the West. To someone normally wracked with humility, this was flattering stuff indeed and no matter how ill deserved one could not help, having a wife at the time who thought me an idiot ass, being somehow grateful for such esteem lifting attention.

'Go ahead Laura, ask him point blank if he's been behind the Iron Curtain.'

'I rather I think should ask you instead Charles, why your fly is very open.'

'O my god. You do know, don't you, how to hit below the belt, Laura. And make one feel utterly buggered and knackered.'

One would have informed Laura that behind the Iron Curtain the caviar, the venison, the brandy and the vodka elixir was superb. Not to mention the tall dark spectacular translator who knew far more English than I did, and who like Laura, but perhaps not as gay and carefree, was admired and pursued following dinner by the merrier Generals and party notables. And at these intimate but sumptuously pleasant gatherings, admittedly I did drop hints at how I thought the East might better coexist with the West. One such deadly serious suggestion getting huge guffaws, that the Soviets secretly mount an unbeatable football team which would challenge and then trounce the winners of the American Rosebowl game.

'Laura I promise you I had no intention of exhibiting myself. I was about in fact to avail of your loo for a pee when you and that agent of espionage happened to come back.'

'And forgive me Charles if I remind you that you have without the merest invitation already peed plenty over this ship without previously availing yourself of the customary facilities for such pissing.'

'God you are Laura, aren't you, very outspokenly unlady-like at times.'

'And you Charles at the moment with your naked feet up on the tea tray are equally awfully quite ungentlemanlylike.'

'Well one has to show one's contempt while in the company of a traitor to the cause of true imperialist capitalism and the natural human truth inherent in such doctrine.'

Notwithstanding Lord Charles's remarks, the amassing of money surplus to one's needs and all the private luxuries it pertained to, was a constant obsession of mine. Despite the bias I did think at the time in Moscow and still do, that my Kremlin solution to a threatening nuclear war was a damn good idea. But for someone to call me a traitor or agent of espionage, good gracious no. However, all that is another story for another time, which, on second thoughts, may indeed, for its heartbreaking romantic intrigues and string of hilarious personal embarrassments, and one accidental unmasking of a major American intelligence operator, be better left untold.

But Laura did nervously fidget at my being accused of espionage and when I point blank enquired of her, she laughingly denied the entire event of the frigate and tender. Plus immediately in the naïve company of Lord Charles, attempting to further inflame his suspicions of me. Making references to the 'Hiyathere', she widened her eyes.

37

'Of course you know dear Charles don't you, that clearly it all adds up. A Chinese girl, or dear me, was it Japanese, escorting the unpatriotic eunuch double agent Commodore back to America where clearly it is intended to create a cell of unconscionably ruthless international triple agents with J.P. here cleverly masterminding it all.'

Lord Charles did rise to the bait but could only mumble unintelligible new accusations, and now seemed far more concerned that he had forgotten to submit his entry giving the number of eggs consumed the previous day aboard ship so that he could win a twenty pound prize. This information being given him by Laura who having successfully guessed the number of eggs consumed on the two previous days, offered him her estimate as she said that with her inside connections aboard, it was not done that she should win the egg guessing contest. But eggs were the least of it, as Charles from an obvious lack of sleep, slumped forward snoring. And full of champagne and gooseberry jam slathered scones, he was finally carried groaning away to his cabin. Shoeless of course, having, while sampling Laura's high heels, pitched his own low ones out Laura's port hole.

As Lord Charles had from the very beginning, everyone now, as we neared journey's end, was letting their hair down. And one could even witness over the deck barriers, the odd first class passenger exchanging comments on the weather with those distinctly in cabin class. Laura, imperturbably in an emerald gown at dinner, and nonchalantly sporting a whole new set of diamond and ruby gems, took the opportunity to elicit last night opinions from the Captain, whose face I was now certain I vaguely remembered from the Game Club. While he appeared to bestow upon me an entirely dismissive attitude, his increasing attentions to Laura were now quite embarrassing in their solicitude.

'Is your caviar chilly enough for you Laura my dear.'

I had in the library checked his entry in 'Who's Who', which described Coast Guard service in the war and his athletic and aviatorial exploits including an open boat rescue he'd made in the Indian Ocean. One did resent his gold braid pressing against Laura's arm. And then, would you believe it, just as my jaws were contentedly idling in the chewing of my grilled Mignon of Tenderloin he even dared contribute a 'Hiyathere' theory. Maintaining in a know it all manner, that the German submarine known to be along the coast at the time, was attempting to kidnap the brilliant atomic physicist and the world authority on cryogenics, and that these staunchly patriotic and courageous gentlemen, with whom he claimed to have once played Bangokok, had attempted to ram the submarine, and in this brave endeavour sank, with a sad conclusion being drawn from the presence of a massive man eating shark known to be in the vicinity.

Needless to say when the Captain so airily mentioned Bangokok, I nearly choked with Laura sending an elbow digging into my ribs. I thought his surmise regarding the Bangokok Boys to be a load of old codswallop. But it was at that exact moment I noticed for the first time that the French professor was absent from his table. Laura having earlier in the evening conspiratorially whispered that she'd received from him at her suite an engraved request for that evening's first dance. And that among the French professor's many distinctions, was not only his membership of the French Academy but also he was expert in cryptography, and a Russian and Japanese scholar.

'Of course J.P. I'm sure he's a member of your New York cell of operatives.'

It was but a second later, just as the Captain was tasting the evening's third wine, that an executive officer with a hurried whisper bent to the Captain's ear. And suddenly the Captain was gone.

'Dear me J.P., wasn't that awfully abrupt.'

I counted, as I looked at her, her five roped necklace of
sparkling cashew sized diamonds and acorn sized rubies. At
which all the other ladies' eyes at table would divert. But
no gems no matter how grand could equal the flashing blue
of Laura's eyes. Or even the splendid saliva on her so white
laughing teeth. Nor for pleasure could they equal the sweet
bouquet of her breath that one craned one's nose forward
to inhale. I was more than somewhat gaga about her. Even
to tying her brassière around my thigh and momentarily
terrifying myself that I could succumb to such a perversion
for the remainder of my life. Of course one was becoming
more and more aware too that Laura in her distinctly
queenly manner, could be a very haughty task master when
she chose. As one sensed she clearly expected to be informed of any shipboard event and was slightly miffed and
mystified at the Captain's sudden disappearance.

'Surely J.P. we couldn't have done anything as awful as
hitting a poor old whale or something. Or do you think my
putting my hand on the Captain's knee was too presump-
tuous of me.'

But only a moment later, the first class Purser was whispering in her ear revealing that a far more horrifying thing
had happened. The French professor in white tie and tails
had apparently disappeared overboard, his plunge into the
waves being apparently witnessed by a seasick third class
passenger trespassing on the first class promenade on the
boat deck. Tears sprang into Laura's eyes and I felt her
fingers squeeze upon my arm as she led me away along the
corridor and out the door to the sun deck.

'O god, J.P. please pray it's not true.'

We stood shivering in the cold breeze as the ship slowed
and reversed engines. As a search was conducted, heads
were craning from lower decks but not another single soul
in first class abandoned the Consommé de Pigeon Sauvage,
or Medaillons de Sole à la Mousse to witness the searchlights
flashing across these endless swells of mountainous tumbling

black seas. The great liner circling for two hours and man-
œuvring to flatten the waves and I'm sure hoping to avoid
bumping the distinguished academic's head should it still
be bobbing on the ice cold waves. Laura refusing to leave
the rails but finally wrapping herself in a black Austrian
loden cape Clare fetched.

'O J.P. the Purser said you can but live at most for twenty
minutes in that cold water.'

The three of us now from the sun deck, staring out into
the hopelessness of this vast heaving darkness. And the
lonely white foam atop breaking waves in the beam of the
floodlights. Laura had taken such pleasure from the professor's distant but frequent attentions. Even Charles, still
drunk as a Lord, his dinner jacket flying open, but his fly
mercifully closed, and wearing slippers gold embroidered
with a fox's head, stumbled to join us.

'What's this I hear of some bloody frog popping into the
drink.'

The withering look Charles got from Laura silenced him.
But with his hand brushing back his blond locks in the
wind he was soon shouting out into the cold night air, a lot
of garbled schoolboy French. Suddenly the floodlights ex-
tinguished and with the increasing resonance of the engines
the ship was on its way again. A tiny bit sobered by the
cold, Lord Charles with further of his sentiments that 'it
was only a Frenchman', lurched after us till disappearing
into the smoke room as I escorted Laura back to her suite
where we sat utterly abject over hot cocoa and biscuits.

'O J.P. he was all alone.'

Lord Charles then rudely barged in, announcing it was
a damn romantic way to die and then asking if anyone
minded his putting it on Laura's bill were he to order some
brandy and champagne 'to buck us all up' as he averred.
Clare having to slap away Charles's hands feeling her as she
was attempting to pack and Laura retiring to her bedroom.
Sitting on her bed, her head quietly resting on my shoulder,

she let roll several big blue eyed tears down her rose tinted cheeks to plummet upon her bejewelled satiny bosoms. One briefly tried to comfort her. Although not easily and indeed rarely given to tears, I too let go with more than a sob. Which really seemed to shake old Lord Charles who came to stand in the dining room doorway, a tulip glass of champagne in his hand.

'I say there, Laura and J.P., aren't you being just a little bit too damn melancholic. Letting some old bookish bugger's nosedive into the old briny ruin all the fun.'

And back in the sitting room as I tried to usher him from Laura's suite, Lord Charles was himself sentimentally mumbling about poor old Bonaparte at the battle of Waterloo whose ruddy bad frog soldiers had let him down. And then after a long dialogue to get him out in the companionway, he was then growling into a half full brandy snifter, something to do with the Duke of Wellington having as a result of that damn battle, a damn nice house perched nicely on London's Hyde Park Corner.

It was a most unnerving and disconcerting last shipboard evening. When I finally retired abed, I consoled myself with Laura's item of underclothing knotted again around my thigh. In the morning following breakfast and a stroll on deck, it was precisely eighteen minutes past twelve Eastern Standard Time when the Ambrose Light Vessel was abeam. And of course what should one see breaking the surface of the waves but the sinister fin of a vast shark cruising alongside. And deep in whose stomach, the French professor, member of the Academy, with his string of degrees after his name, might be. And for all my commiserating with Laura she still would not tell me her address or where she would be.

'J.P. sad as it is, you are a married man. And while one may overlook such things in this little cut off world on the high seas, back on land, I fear one's practical principles are apt to be observed again.'

Every passing minute now I became more forlorn, hating to leave her or indeed even the ship. Wanting somehow to simply stay aboard with her in this womb forever. As indeed one constantly bridge playing dowager did. Only leaving the liner when it went into dry dock. But now as I stood in the chill breeze, the beaver fur of my collar pressed warm on my cheeks, the fabled spires of New York slowly reared up from the western horizon. Piercing all the dreams and carefree beauty of these last blissful days. And less than an hour later, we were slowly moving up the North River, a pale sun briefly flashing down between the canyons of streets of this great soaring city. Then dark clouds. And snow falling.

Last night leaving Laura's suite and divesting myself of Lord Charles into the festive main lounge, I wandered the empty decks in the cold breeze. As I passed the squash court I stood transfixed as I heard from the nearby dog kennels, the long moaning wail of what could only be Clare's Irish wolfhound. Flurries of snow, and inside again in the warmth, the late leavers of the dining room were in loud good spirits, boffing balloons and tearing confetti and quaffing the last of the 'on the house' celebratory champagne. At least I did see as I greeted her that the eyes of the British Ambassador's wife were not unmoist as she said, isn't that so tragic about that so kindly professor.

Finally I stood at the door of the main lounge staring over the heads at where Laura said she first saw me by the grand piano. And on top of which I'd heard Lord Charles had mounted the previous night to scream 'Ôlé' at Laura who evidently had executed a lone and spotlit stunningly electrifying dance back and forth across the floor to bursts of thunderous applause. And just as she had in the middle of my humble state room also electrified me, her body shimmering and vibrating from head to toe.

Now one stared instead at the cerulean blue circles on the brown carpet. One's body aching to touch hers again.

They were singing 'Auld Lang Syne' as I left. And the old hackneyed expression, the show must go on, reminded me that the ship, now making up the time lost searching for the poor professor, had its great massive engines throbbing at full speed ahead. The giant propellers below and beyond these many decks and bulkheads, where Laura brought me to watch the vast shafts turning to thrust and foam a great wide wake on the dark water. To the rhythm of her name. Laura Laura Laura. Making this much the most singularly sad and troubling mystifying journey one had ever made. Filling my heart with an agonizing ache of emptiness. And considerably lengthening and complicating the strange tale of the old Bangokok Boys.

## THE SUMMING UP

New York's grey buildings were clutched together in a bleak white curtain of falling snow as the ship slowly made it's way up the deep flowing Hudson. The ferry crossing to Weehawken. Cars streaming along the shore's highways. Laura's phone busy all morning and I only spotted her on the promenade deck with Clare, rushing her rounds with a sheaf of pound notes, handing out a tip to the deck steward. And all she could do seeing me, was wave and shout a cheery goodbye as I stood watching the Manhattan skyline pass by.

Lord Charles come to take his first peek at the new world was strangely silent. He stood huddled in a black Chesterfield coat and Homburg hat, and on his feet a pair of white tennis shoes. I must confess one did relent a bit in one's resentment, he looked so cold and extremely miserable. I dismally contemplated even risking seeing him again by asking if he had or would have by an extreme chance, Laura's address. Involved in my unpleasant litigation one was not keen to make new friends or indeed even meet some old ones. But as one had previously done on such trips, you forswear to keep knowing one another for the rest of your lives. And as I had learned, you sometimes do meet a day or two later but the old magic of such company rarely revives and you feebly pretend you will somehow somewhere meet again.

Snow swirling along the decks, tug boats nudged the great liner around the tip of the pier and into its Hudson River dock. The ship's massive hawsers slung down and lifted up by stevedores over bollards ashore. Steam throbbed out into the air as the winches turned, the hawsers tightened, and we were finally tied up. With an awfully hollow gnawing loneliness I stood watching passengers collected in the lounges with their passports stamped by immigration officers and waiting to disembark.

On deck while the ship was docking I was not surprised to see uniformed police down on the pier. And half waited for them to rush on board to put Lord Charles in irons for maybe having elbowed the polite little French professor into the drink. For he did the last and previous night run absolutely berserk insane all over the ship. Again getting up to his old tricks, this time perhaps not pounding and kicking stateroom doors of commoners but instead shouting that the great potted palms outside the main saloon needed nitrogenous fertilizer. As he peed down on this hapless vegetation, he was confronted during the urination by the dowager who never left the ship, even in port. And who spent her days between meals being massaged when she wasn't at the card table. This poor shocked lady, with her lorgnette raised and then lowered, became quickly hysterical, and activated the fire alarm. It had to be admitted, the ship's company were endlessly imperturbable and in this instance verbally forgivingly polite, as six of them dragged Lord Charles on his back and by his unslippered feet across the main hall and into the elevator.

Knowing she had a veritable mountain of luggage, I had planned to wait to confront Laura under her Customs letter ashore. But instead of Lord Charles disembarking in custody or even the all socially powerful Laura taking her queenly prerogative as number one down the gang plank, I was astonished to find not only that I was to be the first descending to the pier, but also to be given what one imagined was very important person treatment. Two polite gentlemen ushered me unsearched through Customs and then to be greeted and surrounded by television cameras and reporters. The tallest and thinnest of whom, whose head peeked up over the others, asked was it true that I was the missing link in the riddle of the 'Hiyathere' and the heir to the 'mystery' box.

I was still in my smitten state. Looking back over my shoulder for Laura. And ignoring the questions until I found myself blurting out that I was innocent and would say nothing till I had telephoned my lawyer. Then through the thickening flurries of snow, I again turned to where first class luggage was being stacked under the letter of Laura's surname, G. And one did laugh to see Lord Charles under the letter E, already in some contretemps shouting 'you damned stupid commoner, Bonaparte's coat's in there,' to a stevedore who unceremoniously had, under his letter dumped his luggage for Customs examination, breaking open his case and spilling the meagre contents over the pier.

As I stood in what was to be New York City's first and worst blizzard of the year, I still felt as if I'd just awakened from a lifelong dream. Just managing to smile enigmatically as reporters' questions continued to rain on me from every side. I soon discovered, as his smiling face approached through the little crowd, that my smooth disembarkation and reception ashore was due to the courteous and efficient Lieutenant Alias. Who with one of his detectives holding an umbrella and another showing the way, led me away down the stairs to the street and towards a waiting car.

'I apologize for subjecting you sir to all this attention but at least I hope we made up for it by your being first off the pier. And we'll just have to take it for granted your bags are not full of heroin and cocaine.'

I'd managed a one last look back to see Laura. And she and Clare, with the ship's Purser in tow carrying jewellery and hat boxes, plus three monstrous stevedores behind, lugging her stateroom baggage, were moving down the gangway. My heart dropping into my heels at the thought, in this city of ten million, of ever finding her.

With my bags already aboard I was whisked sirens blaring, to my discreet, albeit fairly sumptuous lodgings overlooking the back of the Frick museum just off Fifth Avenue. The Lieutenant conscious of my worn look, chatted amiably about the restaurants of New York and seemed to know where you could go and get the best lobster, steak, hamburger or fettucini. His detectives popped my bags right in my door. It also became apparent that another mysterious socialite murder had taken place of a fabled rich heiress who'd been an occasional companion of the 'Fourteenth's' and the Lieutenant was in the process of pursuing his early avenues of investigation. The Lieutenant suggesting a meeting on the morrow with the 'Fourteenth's' legacy of racquet and ball.

Bathed in my rather overly ornate pink marble bath and dressed in a thick tweed suit and cap, college scarf around my neck and galoshes on my feet, I went as the snow continued to fall, down Fifth Avenue. Feeling the excitement again of this city. The park a great white apron spreading distantly under the grey stark branches of the trees. Citizens sporting ear muffs in the dry cold and a girl sped by me on skis. My nose was dripping, ears stinging but it was always warmly cheerful to be greeted in the lobby of the Game Club by its old retainers. A familiar face being always so reassuring in this so anonymous city.

'Ah Mr D. Glad to have you back, long time no see.'

I peeked into a nearly empty Great Room with just two elderly gentlemen, one riding the mechanical horse at the canter and another practising golf shots. The instructor, famed for his gymnastic abilities, enquired if I'd like a partner in badminton. But still feeling somewhat stiff with the cold, I went to the baths to recline in the hot room, and to take a Turkish and steam bath. Following this with a swim and power shower I ended up red skinned and glowing. Finally relaxing with a massage, I fell asleep. To wake suddenly with a shivering chill again, from a dream that I was dressing in black tweeds, preparing to go to Laura's funeral.

Darkness outside club window sills piling with snow falling as thick as ever. The gun case as I now referred to the 'Fourteenth's' legacy was just as I had left it at the bottom of my locker. I took a grape juice with soda water and squeeze of two limes and cracker or two slathered with cheese, before going to dine at a cosy little Greek joint around the corner. The waiter I think imagining himself to be presiding in a much grander setting kept solicitously interrupting as I was trying to imagine a conversation I could be having with Laura were she sitting across from me.

'Is everything quite to your satisfaction sir.'

'Yes everything is quite to my satisfaction, thank you.'

With the snow stopped I walked home. Feeling no chill by reliving all my shipboard moments with Laura in my arms. Back in my flat I looked up her surname in the social register, calling the two listed there who seemed delighted by the rude disturbance. And although they were not related and lived out of town in Bronxville and Rhinebeck respectively, both seemed to know of Laura. I then telephoned every decent hotel in New York without success.

Next morning, my cleaning lady's apprentice actor nephew trying his hand at a spot of butlering served me breakfast in the drawing room. The Lieutenant joining me for scrambled eggs smothered in bacon strips remarking how much he admired the oak panelled walls which I informed him were from a famed English manor house. Ensconced over our coffee, jam and croissants in the warmth of my blazing fire, this laconic and strangely professorial looking policeman disclosed that he was obsessed by this baffling case of the 'Fourteenth', and he had learned a lot about the gentleman.

'Of course I speak in the context of a city which has an underground tunnel into the morgue of a funeral parlour where invited guests can amuse themselves in their own inimitable ways. And here we have a guy who went to Yale but that's no crime these modern days. His apartment aside from its being as big as a hotel was one of the most civilized places I've ever seen. He had an impressive library and being a modest book collector myself I know one when I see one. I understand you're in that way of trade.'

The Lieutenant only briefly mentioned the heiress's murder by a hypodermic injection with an instantly lethal sea snake poison, and did not press me with questions but said he had now come to the conclusion that the origins of the 'Hiyathere' mystery could lay somewhere hidden up the blind alleys and corridors of power in Washington DC. By gentle hint he let it also be known that he knew of my presences behind the Iron Curtain. Without mentioning Laura I told of what I'd seen aboard ship. But the Lieutenant's only comment on the Commodore suggested he knew more than he could say.

'I have my way of learning things, the trouble is it's not illegal if all your bills and taxes are paid and you disappear for twenty years. But that's a strange coincidence about the French professor. Curious things happen aboard these big liners. Anyway not many free choices in life but at least suicide is one that's left. That is if the professor wasn't pushed. And without a body to prove it maybe he didn't jump at all.'

While having a third cup of coffee the Lieutenant carefully placed the gun case on a large square of silk and then opened the handsome case bequeathed me by the 'Fourteenth'. Being visibly affected listening to the strains of music emanating from the elegant leather box, and the hushed sad quality of his voice as he read the brass plaque's engraved lettering, and gave a world weary sigh.

'So long as there are no Swiss banking secrecy laws in this town you can find out what's in a guy's bank account, but you can never know what's in his heart. Here's a guy whom you'd be glad to have as a friend. And I hope a person like you, will really go like he says and do something with this. Plus, it's not a bad situation when you can curse anybody who hassles you.'

I had really done everything possible to find out where Laura was. Even telephoning missions for the poor, derelict and destitute. Some of which slammed down the phone thinking I was some kind of pervert when I said the person I was looking for might be in the company of a slightly masculine looking lady. And when I timorously mentioned my dilemma to Lieutenant Alias.

'No problem, if she's in town we'll find her.'

My days now from ten till three were being spent downtown in a dismal courtroom as my lawyers' fees horrifyingly piled up. At least my legal counsel were pleasant well tailored sympathetic gentlemen giving of their best. Who did say that my testimony had one flaw in that it simply reeked of honesty. I needed now to take myself to the Game Club where I could tire my body on the running track, and so, exhausted, regain some kind of momentary peace of mind. And in my despair and anger at this prolonged litigation and on my seventh lap and feeling a sudden trough of desperation, I invoked the 'Fourteenth's' De Alfonce curse upon my adversary. Astonishingly at almost exactly noon the next day, while chewing an apple on the courthouse steps, my whole world of woe seemed to lift totally from my shoulders. And next morning, my lawyer came smiling to pat me on the back outside the doors of the courtroom, to tell me that my legal tormenter of fourteen years duration on three continents, had been forced that very morning to file for bankruptcy. And now modestly elated, I was deeply and fatally depressed again a day later, when Lieutenant Alias briefly called in upon me to report finding Laura and that she sent her love but not her telephone number or address. But as the Lieutenant was leaving he dropped a piece of paper which I picked up to return to him.

'Hey, don't give that back to me. Because I just lost it.'

One's confidence waning I agonized for days, dare I call upon her or telephone. Tortured, imagining her at charity balls and adored at grand dinner parties all over New York, with every man about town who possessed at least one testicle or eye, panting over her beauty and using the other to tabulate the awesome value of her exquisite jewels bequeathed from grandmothers and great grandmothers. And to which I must confess I was not myself entirely indifferent.

Each time passing the Game Club's empty Bangokok court reminded me of that ocean voyage and asleep or awake I was still yearning for her melodic voice, her body's fragrance, the softness of her raven silken hair, or to touch upon the smooth firmness of her balletic alabaster limbs. And haunted by my dream of her death, I each noon day in the frosty air sauntered over the snow down Fifth Avenue to the great sombre marble interior of St Patrick's Cathedral. As atheistically irreligious as I am, I nevertheless lit candles in offering, even attending at Vespers to implore that she would somehow come back to me. Remembering one stormy ocean night her tears wetting my shoulder in the dark. When she said. When I was a little girl and only five years old. They sent me away to school. And Clare was my only little friend.

'Stop, non non. Vous êtes corps à corps, J.P. Encore.'

Even as I did a spot of fencing with sabres with Count Dimitri O'Shawressy der Erzherzog, a not unamusing grandson of a White Russian with a touch of Irish blood, who graciously devoted occasional time as my fencing master, I would imagine, instead of the Count's dark glittering eyes either side of his imposing hawk nose, Laura's laughing face behind his mask. Knowing somehow she probably could, corps à corps or in counter riposte, cut, thrust and pierce me to ribbons. And with sparks flying and the Count screaming his imprecations at my faults, at least in this endeavour I seemed to relieve myself of the legal stresses that tensed my spine and unpleasantly obsessed my brain. Indeed it was damn good practice to be able with a sabre swipe to slice off his shirt and fly buttons, should another Lord Charles turn up in my life. Although concerning the sport, Laura had said, 'I do think J.P. it can be something quite like two gentlemen rather ridiculously standing sparring with their erections.'

Then some days later, having more than once nearly frost bitten my fingers and toes nightly standing across the Avenue in the hope that I would see her, I had just finished a successful fencing session, scoring repeatedly against a brash newcomer, albeit a collegiate champion, when the Lieutenant rang.

'Hey I got a little bit more mystery but also a bundle, so to speak, of not such bad news.'

On the following bitter cold afternoon in the comforting silence of the restaurant lobby of an elegant Madison Avenue hotel, the Lieutenant returned the leather case to me. I was now imitating Laura's habit of taking afternoon tea. Especially celebrating having at last finished my lawsuit. The judge giving judgement in my favour when he refused the liquidator further time to get the money to continue the action. One did not know if this could have had anything to do with the judge being a fan of mine, or the fact of my being such an ineptly honest witness. In any event, I was delighted to sign a copy of one of my books for him and to shake his hand in chambers and to know that the De Alfonce curse really worked.

The Lieutenant rubbing his chilled hands seemed immensely solicitous towards me. As he gave me back the case I could sense he was on the verge of revealing something and then he pulled back. I even thought there was the slightest hint of a curious glad moisture in his eyes. One assumed glad, because few things can make a New York policeman break down in tears. He had also been revisiting the funeral establishment and the 'Fourteenth's' mauso- leum where he had been laid to rest.

'You know I had a funny feeling all the time in there, big as a small church, I kept wondering if our departed friend Horatio's remains were in fact behind the slab. It was as if someone was sort of laughing behind my back. And I tell you what happened before I left that place. I'm thinking of retiring soon. And when I saw these clean comfortable niches, I thought well, you don't feel that if you get put up on a shelf like that, it's absolutely over and done with like being buried in the ground is too final for me. And instead you're there like a book in a library, and you feel maybe one day somebody could take it down again and read it. So I bought a crypt on the spot. My personal niche for the repose of yours truly.'

At the end of our meeting he sat smiling appreciatively swapping riddles with an amiable temporary secretary from Texas accompanying me, who, helping me deal with legal matters, was both refreshingly blunt and also awfully quick on her repartee. And she also seemed dying to know any gruesome facts of the Lieutenant's homicide work.

'Well madam, without going into unpleasant detail, I can tell you this. Every second counts, the sooner you can get to the scene of the crime. The murder victim's head may be battered and his or her body riddled with bullets or stab wounds but before his or her soul vanishes, it can tell you something about what happened in those last moments of life. I wish I was there right at the scene of the perfect suicide when Horatio Josiah De Alfonce got called to higher things. If you start back with the night the yacht dis- appeared, the 'Fourteenth' sure left one real lulu I hope I solve before I retire.'

A detective had come down the soft carpeted steps to whisper in the Lieutenant's ear and he eased himself up out of the dark blue sofa confines. Standing up, and taking off his glasses, he placed his napkin neatly folded on the tea table.

'Sorry to have to leave you and such pleasant cultured company. But someone not so nice just threw a piece of granite off a building and someone below who didn't know it was coming, didn't get out of the way. Plus additionally a well known acting celebrity was just found shot in his bedroom. And O by the way I nearly forgot to give you the bundle of not bad news.'

The Lieutenant put on his horn rimmed spectacles and took from his inside jacket pocket of his dark blue pinstripe suit an envelope for which he asked me to sign a receipt.

'Your Horatio De Alfonce's attache case Mr. D. seems like it's some kind of talisman. Don't forget to take a look in that envelope I just handed you. Found nicely tucked in beneath the velvet and according to the guy's will and his lawyer, it's your property. Goodbye for now. And hope I'll see you soon. And O by the way. I hope all's well with that person whose address was on that little scrap of paper you picked up the other day. You don't meet someone like that but maybe once in three lifetimes.'

In that cosy crimson semi subterranean anteroom upon that memorable afternoon, the envelope the Lieutenant handed me contained, in crisp mint condition, fourteen one thousand dollar bills. I finished counting them just as some late lunching diamond festooned dowagers emerged past and to whom, for obviously delighted reasons, I got up and bowed, much, it appeared to their pleasure. One did feel if not utterly ecstatic, considerably cheered. But for pessimism's sake and the long term equilibrium it provides, I avoided any hilarious handstands or kicking up of heels. Ordering a bottle of Roderer Crystal Brut Champagne of a notable year accompanied by a few nice lubricant grey grains of Beluga. And with my willing Texan lady who

could, according to a brief life history shoot a dozen rattle-
snakes dead in four directions in five seconds, one drank a
copious toast to the 'Fourteenth' and indeed to Lieutenant
Alias who'd made such a sorely needed and pleasant discovery.

My Texan lady hopped in a taxi outside the hotel, heading off home to her husband who was cooking her a spaghetti dinner. I went a long walk north on Madison till
ascending the little hill that descends again to Ninety
Seventh Street. Heading westwards I reached the corner of
Fifth. When a couple of muggers crossed the street out of
the park. Approaching me they began to reach into their
jackets, and I began to reach into mine. I then growled and
bared my teeth snapping. They took a wide detour off the
sidewalk into the middle of the street and ran. One of them,
as he was turning to look back, crashed smack into a parked
car. As the other mugger stood laughing at his prostrate
associate, a private policeman came up behind him and
creamed him equally supine over the head with his club.
Wisely, I thought, I resisted finding the event extremely
amusing.

Back in the reasonable safety of my chambers I did laugh
as I bathed in a thoroughly consoling hot bubble bath.
Donned my silk kimono, pulled on a pair of Game Club
sweat socks and moccasins and dined on some previously
fricasseed chicken. Sitting in front of the fire while smashing back a Bavarian beer, Laura's face created in the flames
and even in the watermark of one of my treasury bills, as I
gazed through this financial vellum mesmerized by its
strangely inconspicuous value. Then while listening to
Fauré's 'Requiem' on a radio station devoted to such things,
the phone rang. Making me jump. And shamed to admit to
oneself a desperate eager anticipation to the identity of that
someone from somewhere who was at last getting in touch
with me. To whom one would also attempt to pretend a
certain blasé indifference.

'You damn bloody commoner.'

'Hello. Who dat dere.'

'You damn well bloody well know in your pidgin English who dat dere is. And you didn't know did you that Laura was one of Britain's first petrol station attendants.'

'As a matter of fact I didn't. But I do wonder why you aren't up a gulch in Nevada where you deserve to be.'

'Well you may as well also bloody well know I deserve to marry Laura and that the major corporations of this bloody country are refusing to employ me. I am in fact being made a menial of. I was a waiter on roller skates. You needn't find that so damn funny. The fact is I've now been demoted to collecting up dirty cutlery and dishes on foot. Nor need you find that so damn funny either. Laura and of course you, much as I hate to admit, are the only ones on this awfully vulgar continent who understand me. Of course I do take an historical comfort from the shabby treatment his fellow frogs meted out to old Bonaparte.'

This was indeed a very chastened sounding Lord Charles but as well as loud jazz in the background there was now also some altercation. Lord Charles as usual and very audibly denouncing commoners. And commoners not being unnumerous in America, some of them must, judging by loud bangs, have been nearby and pronto were attempting to tear the phone out of his hands. While I'm sure his Lordship's feet were contusing them in return in his best imperialist wrath. And the further next sound was clearly that of both phone and wires being ripped out.

Retiring that night, I was tense that I might not now easily sleep. The morrow being one of the rare occasions I had planned to set forth to early brave the world on an ungodly appointment with the barber. And expressly for the purpose of keeping hair out of my eyes under my fencing mask, in an attempt at least, to improve my vision if not my parries and thrusts. Counting my hundredth thousand dollar bill fluttering to earth, finally lulled me to sleep. Only to be jolted awake again, the telephone ringing just as my drawing room big grandfather clock was tolling 3 a.m. I lay ignoring it. But on the persistent thirteenth ring I picked it up, knocking over my bedside water. There then came a sound in my ear that made my private part stiffen like a petrified oak fence post. The gurgling laughter rippling across my brain was Laura's.

'Laura, Laura, Laura.'

As I tried to get her to speak the phone hung up. Leaving me lying awake till dawn, conjuring up the most carnal thoughts and trying to remember where I'd hidden her brassière so I could again tie it around my thigh.

Arising totally exhausted and wobbly of mind, knees and spirit. And of course open to the world's intimidation, my cleaning lady's apprentice actor nephew made me the worst scrambled eggs and coffee of this century but as he also made the morning fire and brought me the newspapers I didn't sack him on the spot. At the barber's my hair was carefully, laboriously and precisely cut exactly the way I emphatically and repeatedly instructed it not to be. Then, so fumingly furious, I was unable to count straight and overtipped him.

'Thank you, have a good day.'

I was sorely tempted to give him a good kick. Rip his ruddy barber's chair to pieces, and pour his lotions down his throat in the manner of Lord Charles. And of course when he saw me fumbling though my thousand dollar bills he was beside himself with ingratiating fingers hysterically brushing infinitesimal specks off my shoulders and with an atomizer, excreting the most god awful men's perfume all over me.

'Make sir smell nice for the ladies.'

But the taxi driver taking me home thought me a raving homosexualist and had the audacity to even suggest we go together to a place meant for that sort of thing and there'd be only half charge on the meter while we were inside.

'Hey fella, what's a matter, ain't I good looking enough for you.'

Determined and resolute to remain hetero, I sent my suit to the cleaner's, took my second bath of the day and with a change of underwear, telephoned Laura's number. After a long pause there was an awfully foreign sounding voice.

'Madam, she so sorry, no take calls. You please send message she read.'

Walking down towards the Game Club that afternoon somewhat forlorn and more nonplussed than ever, I stopped again across the street from Laura's building. Two maids walking dogs came out. And but a mere five minutes later, just as two sleek long limousines pulled up, two unmistakable figures emerged. Into the first car climbed the Commodore and into the second, the oriental lady companion.

As the vehicles pulled away and disappeared in the traffic, I felt a shudder and had an extremely uneasy feeling as I heard numerous sirens in the distance getting closer, and sounding like a city wide alert. Caused I instantly assumed somewhere by Lord Charles. Till suddenly squealing from around all the nearby corners, and streaking up and speeding down Park Avenue, numerous police squad cars screeched to a halt. All in front of me. A veritable sea of blue pouring out of slamming car doors, guns drawn. And pointed directly at yours truly. As I slowly realized in the cold afternoon air, with the sound of nearby windows opening and timid heads peeking out, that I had better raise my hands towards heaven.

'O.K. fella don't move. Turn around. Against the wall. Feet apart.'

While my rights were read to me, I was frisked. Gloves pulled off my fingers and already feeling frostbite on the cold bricks. My ankle paining as my feet were kicked further apart. A shoulder muscle pulled as my arms were suddenly wrenched down behind me and handcuffed.

'Look here, exactly what is the difficulty.'

'Shut up, buster.'

I was protesting in as British a manner as possible, but was unceremoniously bundled into a squad car. Someone had also had an awful lot of garlic for lunch.

At the precinct I was charged with having stolen fourteen thousand dollars and with loitering with intent to commit a further felony. All my lawyers seemed to be away for the day in Washington DC and I was thrown into a cell. It was not till past midnight, when a sergeant with nothing better to do, was snooping further in my wallet, happened upon Lieutenant Alias's card. And a phone call later, I was released, brought a hot cup of coffee and doughnut and profusely apologized to.

Not a further peep from Laura nor did I dare loiter again across from her building. But crossing Fifty Eighth Street by the Plaza Fountain I at least ran into an old girlfriend and for a few pleasant nights headed with her to the opera and ballet. She also took a few round trip rides with me on the Staten Island ferry, something I religiously did at least twice a week. Simply to watch from the stern of the vessel the tip of Manhattan shrink against a vast American sky. Feeling for a few moments cleansed of the island's intimidating brooding turmoil distilled from all its silent scurrying lives.

Although I could not stop thinking of Laura, my days had now assumed again the sort of dull, albeit celibate, normality I preferred. However my old girlfriend on the arrival of her monthly alimony cheque suddenly departed for Palm Beach and I returned to my lonely walks in the park and zoo. Also visiting to sit by the leafy grotto in the conservatory of the Frick Museum. And this afternoon as I sat on a stone bench watching the bronze frogs spouting their little fountains of water out their mouths, something made me look up. My heart pounding, I felt the hair stand stiff on the back of my neck. For there in the shadow of the cloister across from me, in a morning suit, opera hat and cane, was standing the French professor.

By the time I could gather my senses and jump up, the figure had turned and disappeared into the large gallery. I crossed the courtyard conservatory, mounted the steps and followed. A mother and a small girl were there just inside the door and a uniformed museum guard down at the other end of the room. I raced from gallery to gallery, to finally question the attendants at the door. They stoutly denied seeing anyone of the description I gave and politely informed me that no one unless crippled was allowed in the museum carrying a cane.

I had the next few days the uncomfortable feeling I was being followed. I even nipped in and out of the subways and jumped on and off trains. Lieutenant Alias was up to his teeth in murders but left a message he would be in touch as soon as he could. Lying late abed over breakfast with the Daily News and New York Times till eleven, and scribbling odd notes on the state of my middle aged dilemma of perhaps now seeing things, I even seriously toyed with a suggestion from the actor nephew of my cleaning lady that I write him a one act play in which he could star.

'You see Mr D. the plot could be about an actor doing a spot of butlering for an aged extremely rich curmudgeonly old fogey who was slowly beginning to lose his mind, with the butler desperately trying daily to get him to change his will in the butler's favour before the old gent was finally declared incompetent.'

Of course had he not been such a depressingly piss poor butler and had I not recently banked fourteen thousand dollars, one might have entertained the idea as a very promising farce and something to enthusiastically tackle. But this young blond matinee idol type spent half his time when he thought I wasn't looking, grinning and gesticulating to himself in the drawing room mirror and scrutinizing the stock exchange pages of my newspaper. He was also borrowing my clothes for his auditions, using my toilet waters and I actually caught him when he thought I'd departed for the day, taking a bubble bath which I wouldn't have minded so much except it was with my special goat's milk preparation given me by Laura. And then ten minutes later when he'd dressed, polishing his shoes with one of my cashmere sweaters. The latter yellow and his shoes black.

'I say there my good man, that happens to be an article of my personal clothing.'

'Sorry my dear employer but I happen to be in a hurry. I'm tap dancing in an audition for a Broadway musical.'

Just as the last snows of the year's first blizzard had finally disappeared, snow began to fall again on this Monday early afternoon. Soothingly having spent the weekend in Boston taking walks around Back Bay and Beacon Hill and visiting my publisher, I was feeling chipper as I munched an apple out my door. Now avoiding the Frick entirely and instead, going slumming, taking my usual walk on the West side down Columbus Avenue before retiring early to the Game Club due to the inclemency. I had just finished my fencing session and elbows resting on the high sill, was staring out the window at the snow falling in the park. While I listened to the Count on the telephone instructing his broker to sell a massive block of shares which were just about to peak. And right at that moment, reasonably calm despite the black smears on my yellow cashmere sweater, I there and then decided to return to Europe for the rest of my life. Andorra being a nice little cosy location And to be even there laid to rest. As I walked with the Count from the fencing room, I was already planning to board a plane by the weekend.

'Ah but my dear Jay Pee, but of course no, not, never. How could you ever think in your correct senses to leave this bourse of a city where one can buy murder or love, or sell souls or diamonds. With its good telephones, restaurants and stock exchanges. Plus this marvellous club where some not at all bad looking women with some not very bad legs nor buttocks socially come more than occasionally. Who indeed will be in plenty supply next week at the Metropolitan Championships.'

It was entirely true, that never in my life had I ever seen such a collected set of singularly beautiful women attend anywhere as those who showed up even at the most insignificant Sabre Championships. I once enquired of one such lady why this should be. And was told it was because fencers, like ballet dancers, developed such marvellous gluteal muscles which discerning females found desirable to admire. One remembered, as perhaps being closer to the truth, Laura's remark, of fencing resembling sparring with erections. But it did made me think twice of the Count's advice as I went into the chiropodist's office for a toenail cut and corn treatment.

When reclined on the green setee in the Game Club baths I still had the dilemma of my departure on my mind. Watching in the one hundred and forty degree heat, the clock hand sweep away a further fifteen minutes of my life. It was utterly amazing, just how, just ten previous mornings ago one's previous wife intimated in a letter, that I was all washed up. And how fast, in the face of such demoralizing ridicule, did one's last vestige of optimism disappear. And I found myself composing an ad for the lovelorn personal column of a thought to be sophisticated reasonably popular journal.

Recently rejected by sublimely beautiful and sublimely rich heiress, separated and only slightly maritably encumbered, nearly completely pale white male of mature age, booked on a weight reducing cruise from which intends suicide by drowning and now resigned to being miserably desperate and further disappointed during last few weeks of life, wants to meet uncreative mildly stupid and even slightly ugly, non career girl (poverty no hindrance), who unable to do better, but whose marvellous mother mercifully taught her cooking and sewing, will appreciate the drawbacks of grey balding, tending towards mild perversions, and mid section avoirdupois, and whose present stammering pomposity is due to repeated but non violent business reverses (two bankruptcies and one long court case recently settled), and the victim of marriage (two nearly violent divorces and two current alimonies), and who has, thank god, no sense of humour, (which he feels encourages people to take further advantage of him) and who absolutely beyond any doubt detests and distrusts anyone claiming one, and who hates travelling, candle light dining (preferring curmudgeonly reflection and licking of wounds) and who has cockroaches but no bedbugs, fleas or lice in quite a decent apartment (previous wives and their boyfriends took previous two really decent houses) plus there is a would be half arsed butler who collects mail and serves breakfast and whose aunt cleans up. If you would like to meet me for a brief future together, bring your own coffin.

I roused myself, from recalling my literary effort and the attendant editorial difficulties on the telephone in its placing, to now go perch on a bench in the steam room and then take a cold shower and dive into the pool. I stayed swimming underwater in the green tinted depths, thinking while I wiggled my fins, that although a wise man does not trust confidence too far, nevertheless a modest amount is required for a butler to think one deserves decent service. Dangerously delayed in the depths of the swimming pool by such unesteeming thoughts, I surfaced just in the nick of time gasping for breath and then heard for the first desperately welcomed moment in years, my name paged to the telephone.

My legs sent the water boiling behind me as I dug my arms slashing to the end of the pool. Climbed the indented marble ladder, skinning my knee. Grabbing a couple of towels in which to wrap, I hurried, blood dripping, to the pair of mahogany kiosks where I dialled O and sat soaking wet on the seat, panting. Now listening, and waiting for a voice, which was that of the charming Game Club operator who flatteringly recognized mine.

'Mr D. hold on I have someone just coming on the line for you.'

Then came a desperate long silence. And no small amount of pessimism tinged with despair. And just as I was about to hang up, concluding, that as usual, it was all a mistake, the previous wives were right, no one wants, if they ever did, to get in touch with me anymore. There came that unmistakable gurglingly amused, erection provoking laughter, and blissfully, finally after all the waiting lonely weeks, Laura's voice.

'J.P., J.P. it's me. Inviting you for drinks.'

As soon as I'd confirmed the address which I already knew by heart and harrowing experience, and before I could say even a word of fond greeting, the phone hung up. But together with my still dripping hair I was weeping tears of ecstasy. And the towel over my lap was out like a tent. For this latter reason one had to remain sitting till one was again calm between the legs. Due to the nudity in this very masculine sporting gentleman's club, the nature of one's provocation to tumescence might easily be misunderstood.

Snow was now falling thickly and piled high along the streets by ploughs churning by. The evening's sidewalks had turned icy, but I never walked up along Fifth Avenue with such a light footed step. Nor turned towards Park through these crosstown streets, with one's heart soaring with such joy. Only wrapped in my college rowing pink, my butler having gone off to his audition in my mackintosh, I was overcoatless. But even so I was tingling warm under my tweed waistcoat and alive to every colour, every passing doorway and every face. Suddenly seeing the world friendly around me once again. Taking comfort in passing these great stone edifices in which so many dowagers comfortably and anciently lived celebrating much of the mighty wealth of this nation.

On the corner I stopped to dig some snow out of the side of my shoe. Clapping my hands for warmth and looking once more at this address across from which I was arrested. Only a hop skip and jump away from my own lodgings, but so many impossible miles of yearning between. I stared up at where the top floors terraced back and then suddenly I was touched on the shoulder.

'Do please excuse me, but weren't we on the same ship coming over. Would you mind if we walked along together.'

I was incredulous. Here was this total stranger on a snowy street corner. The man with those words and similar ones following, wanting to know awfully desperately where I was going. I suppose one cannot trust one's own behaviour but I actually ended up being polite. Being at least bucked a bit, being recognized by someone, having had for so many years been severely reminded by one's wives using their favourite expression, 'Who the hell has ever heard of you or knows who the hell you are.' But I had finally to assume, as he kept stepping in front of me, that I was being deliberately delayed. Especially as I could over his shoulder swear I was seeing the French professor in opera hat, cloak and cane emerge from Laura's building and quickly before I could get any closer, be whisked away in what looked like an awfully bullet proof limousine.

'Get the bloody hell out of my way.'

I managed to shove the gentleman off the curb and ankle deep into a snowdrift. And made for the canopy of Laura's entrance to enter through two sets of doors, one sliding and obviously inches thick with bullet proof glass and into the reddened welcoming glow of a fire and the lobby's warmth.

'Good evening sir. Whom do you wish to see.'

Two plinths with stone greyhounds on their haunches flanking the blazing logs framed by a black marble chimney

piece. The panelled lobby possessed of a distinctly Eliza-
bethan motif. A large refectory table with a visitors' book.
A wave of homesickness for Europe overcame me. More
painful for knowing so indelibly I was still in New York.

I was beginning to more than think one was entering a
military installation as one doorman nearly required my
passport and letters of credit from the Morgan Guarantee
and Trust Company. I was tempted to suggest might they
also need several references preferably from an Episcopalian
bishop. But after much confab on his intercom system I
was finally shown along the black and white marble hall to
a private elevator. Then one of his two associate doormen,
looking at the visitors' book, called after me.

'You wouldn't be now, would you an imposter of the
great man himself.'

Had one of my present or previous wives been with me,
to have even deigned venture an answer, I'd have been
accused of an egotism bordering on insanity. Although I
cast no aspersion on such condition, always having found
folk having taken a long sabbatical from their senses to be
eminently sensible. However I'd made the dreadfully
slightly conceited mistake, of not only framing the 'Fourteenth's' letter to me and putting it up over my chimney
piece, but of also sending copies of it to my present and
previous wives. Now in this present pleasantly welcoming
lobby I did stop in my tracks and stare back at this concierge
smilingly waiting for an answer.

'Sure you're not are you the great man himself.'

Having had, at unfriendly interrogations, taken the surly
veiled abuse of opposing lawyers who described me as anything but great, I certainly did not know how to take this
comment. Indeed I'd been accused of being an international
litigator bringing innocent corporations to their knees.
However one also had to be certain it was not another of
Laura's little jokes similar to those she arranged aboard
ship, so I demurely replied.

'I wish I were the great man, but in fact all I am is a cousin.'

'Ah well give us your autograph then, we'd be grateful. Sure there'd be a bit of the same blood in your veins.'

I duly signed the various scraps of paper put in front of me with my surname and the initials T.J. And then shown out on the ninth floor I duly tripped on the thick rug into an ante room furnished in French Empire, and the walls covered in the rather macabre cautionary drawings of a famed cartoonist. In a corner, a collection of polo mallets and canes. And as I waited I dared look at the labels affixed to boxes of gifts and flowers each inscribed to Laura, with endearments and signed by some gentleman's name. I agonized wondering which of the fawning bastards might be in receipt of her favours. Even to imagining bloated hairy disagreeably lecherous toads, pressing their lips and misshapened weight upon her own soft sunny lips and lissomly exquisite body.

I was caught twisting one of the more ornate cards into a pretzel just as a door finally opened and an elderly grey haired uniformed maid appeared. Who summoned me in a strong Scottish accent to follow her. I was nervously shaking like a leaf as we walked over a soft deep pile carpet along a hallway of Audubon drawings and arrived in a marble floored rotunda, off which four doors opened, and the lower walls of which, like strange eyes staring at one were hung with several works of painters, Klimt and Klee. The maid now ushering me through one of the doors. Where I found myself in the hush of a large sound proofed panelled library. A wood fire blazing in a black marble fireplace. Asked to wait, I perused the shelves amid many obviously valuable editions, and my heart suddenly began thumping. To realize I was in none other than the 'Fourteenth's' private sanctum. A years old photograph of him in yachting cap, next to the Commodore and both smiling on the stern deck of a vessel which could only have been the 'Hiyathere'.

'May I get you a drink sir.'

'No thank you.'

'Miss Laura shall be with you presently sir.'

This time a young black maid, astonishingly also with Scottish accent, was quickly gone again, and I busied myself reading titles on these elegantly leather bound tomes. To find tucked away at the end of a shelf, my own paltry output. Or as the French put it, one's œuvre, of regrettably recently out of print books. But here they resided flatteringly gold embossed and morocco bound. That the 'Fourteenth' was extremely rich there could be no doubt, just judging from the elaborate apartment and a few of the Meissen statuettes on the chimney piece.

By the minute more haunted and by the second more anxious to see Laura, I sat down sinking deep on the brown velvet softness of the sofa. Under the lamp on the table next to me, the surface of which was inlaid with scenes and figures from the tarot, was an anthology of poetry and underneath that a yesteryear copy of a prep school year book, through which I went paging. Among photographs in the back I was astonished to see one of the 'Fourteenth' with members of the school lacrosse team among whom were some of the vanished faces of the 'Hiyathere' thirteen. Here they were, together, side by side, on a playing field in this sylvan setting. Where in fact, in the Navy, I had myself been at school overlooking the Susquehanna River and a town called Port Deposit in Maryland. I vaguely remembered seeing many years previous the same photograph once displayed in the Game Club trophy room.

A ship's clock suddenly clanged four bells behind me, and I turned, my eyes fixing upon a bronze replica of the 'Fourteenth's' hand, and once more my recently barbered hair at the back of my neck stood up on end. Just as the dark complexioned maid returned to summon and lead me back into the rotunda and then into what seemed a tiny sitting room, full of bric à brac and mementoes and photographs of a woman in every imaginable kit from foxhunting to safari, from polar expedition to tennis. And I did venture to ask of the lady's identity.

'Aye, they are pictures of Mr De Alfonce Adams' mother. Wasn't she beautiful.'

Then a secret hidden door in the wall silently opened and we stepped into a small exquisitely panelled elevator, rising slowly upwards through three further floors above. My heart thumping to finally step out and be left on a balcony which looked down into a vaulted high ceilinged room. And there beneath a crystal chandelier in grass green tennis clothes, her face laughing, her beautiful legs astride on what appeared to be an original Bangokok court, stood Laura. In her hand, swooshing it back and forth, a racquet identical to the ones bequeathed me by the 'Fourteenth'. Impossibly glad to see her, I could feel the blood drain from my temples and my privates tingle alive between my legs.

'Well J.P. Please don't just stand up there looking so nonplussed and stupefied. Suitable garments you'll find just to your right behind you and through that door, and where you may also dress.'

Speechless I did remain but much thoughtful, dreaming as I delightedly looked at her there, that she might be the mother of a whole lot of little Lauras and Jay Pees that I might provoke in her should the gods only bestow such fortune upon me. But just as swiftly I had to turn away, my trousers embarrassingly and painfully out like a tent. Escaping into the marble mirrored dressing room where black and green tile shelves were full of scents, bath salts, towels, and where a glass enclosed shower had spouts from all directions, even underfoot. And laid out were my size in whites and sneakers and a De Alfonce Tennis case, which with the exception of the dedication brass plate, was identical to my own from the 'Fourteenth'.

As I descended dressed and holding the same strange shaped racquet bequeathed me by my benefactor, Laura stood volleying the strangely hushed pneumatic ball against an end wall. On a console table, four tulip glasses and a bottle of champagne in a silver wine cooler.

'J.P. you look as if you've seen a ghost.'

'As a matter of fact I rather think I have.'

'You mustn't imagine it all so odd. But isn't it quite miraculous you should have known my uncle. And since you've inherited his quite nutty game I thought you wouldn't mind my beating you ragged at it. Are you ready to do battle. I propose that since the ceiling chandelier interferes with lobbing that it and the ceiling are in play. Clare will be umpire.'

In this astonishing apartment clearly the vast room was a ballroom. Now all geared out with a Bangokok court identical to the Game Club's. And of course, who should remain dramatically lurking smirking in a doorway opposite, face shaded by the visor of an American baseball cap, but Lord Charles. Who now gigglingly emerged to attend upon and pop the champagne cork.

'And J.P. of course I'm sure you'll approve of Charles being line judge.'

If the way Charles was quickly, and carelessly as usual, spilling the wine foaming all over the glasses and table and was already gulping the contents of his own glass down, this was to be clearly one hell of a disputed match on line calls. And I was not wrong in that assumption. When closeness allowed, Charles called my acing thunderbolt serves out and many of Laura's lobbing top spin baseline shots in. Provoking me to one of the few tantrums of my life.

'You cross eyed bugger you.'

'Look here you commoner, no fucking foul language on court please.'

Clare with the maid in attendance, sitting up in a balcony at one end of the room umpiring was at first reading a book, until suddenly, as the tight match turned into a titanic struggle, she too became engrossed.

'I say this is a jolly marvellous game to watch.'

I was as fit as a fiddle hitting running forehands down the line in response to Laura's sliced back hand near winners. And swallowing down a glass of champagne every time we changed courts. And another bottle of champagne was soon opened with Lord Charles that eternal young son of a bitch aristocrat actually proposing a toast to my efforts.

'Good show J.P., pity you're not up to Laura's calibre but damn good show all the same.'

Upon that court that night was enacted the first rudimentary game of De Alfonce Tennis. In which I unbelievably beat Laura in the middle set, losing the first and last. As we further quaffed the now celebratory third bottle, and with Laura summoned to the telephone, I reminded Charles of his middle of the night phone call which seemed to make him cower sheepishly to a distant corner where he disappeared. I did laugh however when he reappeared, wearing an American football uniform, the large lettered word Tome on the jersey.

'Regardez moi, you commoner.'

Obviously the uniform was from one of the 'Fourteenth's' closets. And it transpired that Laura, that very day had visited his crypt with a bouquet of wild flowers, commenting that few European monarchs had a mausoleum nearly so grand. And Charles now, looking like some monster from Mars, was busy refilling glasses.

'Let me yet propose another toast to your outstanding performance J.P. one wouldn't think by it that you were at all middle aged and over the hill.'

As it happened the unflattering Lord Charles was, if not a good referee, a jolly damn generous host with other folk's champagne. Indeed by his fifth glass of wine he was averring to have become somewhat a fan of mine and actually claiming to have read something I wrote. Clare whom I had hardly ever much heard speak before actually backed him up but stabbed me with a pang of jealousy as it became apparent that Charles was in fact residing in these very apartments.

'Got to eat some of my words J.P., obviously there are one or two of these Americans who do know how to lay on a modicum of the old creature comforts.'

One was then further stunned to learn that both he and Laura, unbelievably, had till a day or two previously, been working in the same restaurant where Laura was a waitress on roller skates.

'J.P. I so adored it. Always wanted to be one. Our English accents got us enormous tips. Such fun. Charles was a flop of course.'

'I most certainly was not. I quit in disgust at being demoted to bus boy. I mean to say sorting dishes on foot for the dishwashers is simply beneath my dignity.'

'But dear Charles what on earth did you expect, having attempted your so called impeccable Olympic pirouette and dizzily spinning out of control on your arse, you did dump so many sauce soaked dishes on so many people's heads.'

Following our marvellous electrifying game which left me stunned and elated by its sheer enjoyable pleasure to play, and having showered, dressed and reappeared to await the descent of Laura to one of the downstairs salons, I actually found myself purring. Laura flowed in laughing in a tweed tartan skirt of some noble clan. A cameo at the neck of her chaste long sleeved beige silk blouse. Beneath which her breasts were gently shaking and upon which I so longed to again press my lips and fingers. The devilment so sparkling in her blue eyes. And the rainbow colours glinting in the chandelier seemed to descend to shine on her black hair.

'Ah J.P. isn't it. Just like old times being back aboard ship again. The four of us sitting here assembled.'

Another bottle of champagne served with a veritable cauldron of caviar and smoked delicate varieties of other fish. A fire blazing in the grate reflecting up around the walls on portraits, seemingly of the 'Fourteenth's' relatives,

with one of an exquisitely beautiful woman in a black ball
gown enigmatically staring from a pair of bright blue eyes,
who was Laura's mother. And as I sat looking at Laura and
bathed in the warm exquisite vowels of her voice, the soft
faint soothing strains of Janáček's 'Opus Seventeen' in
the background, the next hour or so became the most con-
tented of my entire life.

'Ah but J.P. New York is so ruthlessly exciting, one can't
get quite enough of it. Everyone either thinks they're so
important or else so insignificant. But the wonderful thing
is that the insignificant get a chance to think they are so
important. And for their few minutes of glory they can then
be such marvellous fun and so blatantly confident that they
blithely walk over you. I love it. But even so one is moving
on. Towards the Grand Canyon J.P., and all that tourist
sort of thing. Isn't it quaint, Charles here is delivering
someone's brand new Rolls Royce to them in Los Angeles.
We're leaving first thing in the morning.'

Had I a moment to plead alone I would have begged her
to hole up with me in Andorra till death do us part or one's
suing wives' lawyers bankrupted me. But unnervingly each
time Laura looked at me she would suddenly burst into
nearly uncontrolled fits of laughter. Having wasted weeks
in my contemplative desperation over her, I somehow knew
I needed time to shore up my affairs and represent my case
to her anew, before tackling following her to the Pacific
ocean and maybe even oriental places due west and the
beyond.

'Come J.P. let me show you our little digs.'

For more than an hour we toured the apartment extending through four entire floors and covering nearly thirty
rooms and three different kitchens. I noticed as we passed
through some doors that they both opened and closed automatically in front and behind one with a very ominous and
heavy thud and click indeed. Charles occupying a bedroom
certainly fit for a lord, with not only two bathrooms but

also a dressing room, and a personal salon with a gothic stained glass windowed chapel en suite. Upon the use of which he was delighted to enlighten me.

'Of course you know J.P., aristocrats don't pray to God they rather confer with him.'

In the course of the tour and viewing some photographs, I discovered Laura had also inherited a 30,000 acre ranch in Nevada to which Charles boasting of his equestrian expertise said he would pay a visit.

'I'll show your ranch hands Laura a thing or two about roping a steer.'

And at the moment of departure downtown for a spaghetti dinner Charles would not remove his football uniform. He did however, as we all four ventured out, borrow the 'Fourteenth's' overcoat. The evening had the sad yet excited overtones of one's Christmas eves one had known growing up in this land, where each move and moment was full of precious portent and no moment was to be overlooked in its savouring. At least while Lord Charles was behaving.

It transpired that that blue blood's lack of outer wear came of his not realizing this was a city where it was every man for himself. Charles had in a snowfall upon coming across his first citizen prostrate in the gutter, taken off his coat to cover this desolate outcast.

'And do you know what bloody well happened J.P., I was summoning help when another bloody bastard came along, examined my coat from a damn good tailor, and snatched it up off this poor frozen bugger and ran.'

But such humanity I knew, would not be lost upon Laura. Whose invitation and prospect of departure already had me fast sinking deep again into hauntingly painful bowels of loneliness. She had, it seemed, taken to caring for the errant Lord Charles in a way I would rather wasn't so matey. He of course was only too ready to let me know how utterly content he was in the lavish confines of her company. Even the shy silent Clare, as we finished our game, stepped down from the balcony to take my arm as if to comfort me.

'You know J.P. just as you won the second set, you mustn't give up on Laura.'

The heavy glass doors clicking behind us, we were ushered out by all three doormen to a large limousine awaiting us at the door. Departing south towards the lights towering over Grand Central Station at the foot of north Park Avenue, with yet another bottle of champagne in tow. Driving along the ramp around the bleak walls and massive windows of this railway building, Laura in her black Austrian loden cape seemed very quiet and distracted. While Charles kept up his banter, both demeaning and flattering.

'You know J.P. Laura tells me you are an extremely clever chap. Now how do you, with your singularly banal origins and birth, account for that.'

But Charles did have something chaotically likeable about him. And as the night progressed and I suppose we grew drunker, one did finally exchange what might be described as endearments. And as we stood taking a pee together in the latrine of one of the bars in our pub crawl, one also became strangely cautious.

'Ah J.P. you're a fucking brick. No I don't mean prick. Brick in the best English sense of that word. Of course I know you must be an espionage agent. And Laura tells me you really do rub elbows with the high and mighty in the Kremlin.'

It was as if Laura, in the certainty of knowing what I did, might be more than just the laughingly gay carefree girl she seemed. However wherever we went this night, we were delicately extricated by her whenever Charles's misbehaviour invariably resulted in our being refused admission or if momentarily admitted then promptly thrown out. He even had us facing what might have been guns in one mafia establishment, when swarthy persons were reaching under their jackets as Charles, exercising his American slang, loudly announced.

'This slimy joint is fit only for slobs.'

Two killer dons rose from their table to approach us. But at the intervention of Laura the pair of swarthy gents suddenly seemed willing to forgive us anything. Especially if Laura would ditch us and join them in Phoenix, Arizona where they were flying the next day. And as a waiter loaded down under a stack of dishes, waited patiently to get by, they continued their imprecation.

'Hey baby, why is a beautiful classy lady like you and your girlfriend here wasting your time with just a couple of jerks.'

Upon these words Lord Charles's foot seemed to come from nowhere. Rising up between these two gangsterish gents to kick the waiter's full tray straight up to the ceiling. From where it rained down Chianti, fettucini and copious olive oil over the entire restaurant. The two mafia dons seemed less to mind their customers turning red as much as they did their table cloths becoming spotted pink.

'Hey look what he done to the fucking linen, I'll kill him.'

The ladies screaming and tables upset, both mafia gents went for Lord Charles, who with two of the most utterly brilliant sizzling left and right hooks I've ever seen delivered, laid the pair of them out flat unconscious on their backs. Even two henchmen making their way towards us, stopped. If not in terror at least in awe. And I even had the temerity to shove a plate of hot pasta up into a nearby snarling protesting elderly waiter's face. In the utter three second silence that ensued, we all four, with Charles taking up the rear and still mostly attired in his American football uniform, but now sporting on top of his helmet one of Laura's Ascot bonnets, backed us out of the restaurant. And into the ominously temporary safety of First Avenue.

'I say girls do please bloody well be quick, won't you, they've got guns out.'

Shoved into the limousine and our chaffeur terrorized, we were gone in a cloud of exhaust and swirling snow. Taxi cab drivers blaring at us as our wheels skidded and slid us all over the road. And there was no doubt whatever in my mind that remaining in the company of Lord Charles much longer would get if not all of us, at least me reposing on a cold slab in Bellevue morgue. Which practically happened ten minutes later, stopping at a bar to soothe our nerves. Where, when a cockroach sped along the edge of the table, Charles took a full bottle of Scotch whisky to smash the offending insect into an alcoholic kingdom come. And then reminded everyone protestingly present.

'You bunch of ungrateful buggers, you swindled this island of fourteen thousand acres from the Indians and now you've got bloody filthy bugs all over the place.'

Finally sometime after midnight down some steps in a bar on the southern edge of Greenwich village, peace at last reigned. With Laura and Clare wisely drinking mineral water. But Charles obtaining for the two of us repeated free drinks of an exquisite Armagnac from a friendly bartender. Who'd whispered to Charles that not only had he heard of me but had actually read some of my scribbles. Although far from being dangerously ready to explode with conceit, this news did of course have the effect of going straight to swelling my previously long humbled head.

'By jove J.P. it's ruddy wonderful you're not a stuffed shirt, you old fart, after all.'

And with about my seventh shot of ancient Armagnac, the bartender, Charles and I were, arms around each other's shoulders, standing on top of the bar, attempting as an out of tune threesome, to sing as a quartet. And the very last thing I remembered of the evening was Laura later leaning across the table, smilingly taking my hand, a yearning sadness in her quiet voice.

'O I do so wish I could tell you everything J.P.'

My next clear memory was being shaken back to life by

77

Austin early afternoon in my lodgings. Although I could vaguely recall embracing a tearful Laura, and vaguely swearing lifelong friendship with Clare and Lord Charles. I was now after a night of semi nightmares of my teeth breaking into pieces and falling out of my mouth, feeling morally exhausted. But just as I woke I was dreaming of playing on a Bangokok court with Laura, both of us dancing on great billowy clouds, our feather light racquets held like batons and conducting in slow motion a great thousand voice choir singing Gounod's 'Ave Maria'. And the soothing sounds of those orchestral swelling voices made me wake whispering over and over the name.

### De Alfonce

Suffering one of the worst hangovers of my life, I quaffed glasses of fresh grapefruit juice. And I found the De Alfonce Tennis case I'd used at Laura's delivered outside my door with a card,

### From Laura
xxx

I felt my way out into the street to summon a taxi to the Game Club. And arriving there, paused in the lobby to ring her number, forlornly to find all three had left westwards only minutes before in the brand new Rolls Royce. And in Lord Charles's hands, god help that innocent vehicle.

It took me nearly three full days of steam baths, and cold spout power showers to clear my head and recover from triple vision, wobbly legs, and throbbing head. My butler Austin, failing to be cast in his musical, was now spending infernal and irritating practice bouts in the pantry, tap dancing for another audition in a black minstrel show. But he did manage in between sessions to fetch up and open a large parcel, just as I was finishing drying myself and

donning my polka dot underwear which he was enviously
eyeing. And as I stood deliberating as to what he'd left me
to wear he dumped a batch of mail on my bed.

'Ah we are popular this morning sir, aren't we. And while
you were in the bath, Lieutenant Alias called by to say that
this telephone is being tapped.'

My paranoia, already extremely inflamed needed only the
replies I now faced from my lovelorn ad to maybe pop me
into permanent orbit. One regretfully recalled the sheer
frustrated desperation which possessed me to publish it.
And one was terrified opening each envelope that some embittered feminist would be any second pounding on my
door with a shotgun. I could hardly bear to view the several
accompanying colour photographs. But having fully deserved these consequences, and out of one's gentlemanly re-.
gard, I forced myself to view and read every word of every
single reply. Fourteen as it happened and all of which smell-
ed of mediocre perfume and were mostly in the vein of:

I know that you're not trying to sound rich and sort of
wonderful but nobody could be that bad which could
mean you're better than most bastards, and I more than
might be just the wonderful girl for you. That's not the
real me you're seeing, because since that picture was
taken I have lost forty six pounds.

Then at nearly the bottom of the pile of replies there was
an unperfumed vellum envelope sealed with a family crest
in red wax and printed in a neat black ink. The letter inside
was on engraved handmade paper, from an address in Rock-
land County, New York State.

Hawthorne Manse
Echo Park
Dear Curmudgeon,
    Hi ya there, you must be the first human being in
tortoise years, I feel I can really write to. My name's

Julianna but everybody calls me Julia. I know right away
I'm sounding banal but listen. You sound reasonably civilized and I have been looking all my life for a really
insanely humourless fellow like you but I happen to be
all the wrong things you require. Like intelligent, beautiful and rich and with a ballet trained body which over
the years (24) has been much tensile tested (those last
two words just came to mind). My lifelong problem has
been, being smarter, richer and a better linguist than all
the men I have ever met, and maybe that's why your
sublime heiress threw you over, (but who knows she
wasn't playing hard to get) but I am a softie romantic
and unfortunately also an inverted snob from one of
Boston's nearly best families (which I admit is not saying
much these days). I trained for the ballet but broke both
my arms in a fall and so took up and promptly broke a
leg foxhunting and although I dislike admitting so, I now
only hunt for men. Woof woof. (That's me barking). And
I would be gleefully glad and more than mildly ready to
pervert you. I can't cook, or sew but at least, speaking of
cooking, I did try to poison my second husband. (Yes
you guessed it, he was thinking of poisoning me). I
dropped a mushroom in the pot when I thought the cook
wasn't looking, but she was, and luckily didn't like my
husband either. Anyway we both got caught and I play
Brahms and Faure here, where I've been sent for six
months. I know you're only joking but what I really do
have, is my own coffin. Imagine what, with the real dirty
mind I absolutely know for certain you've got, you might
do to me in it. My god it doesn't bear thinking about
We really could frolic in a suicide pact together all the
way to the grave.

JULIA

P.S. Don't be put off by this address. It is in fact (as you
may have soberly guessed) a mental institution but only

for the non criminal and very brightest and richest people. My apartment here is private and visiting is anytime. In fact this tea time Saturday afternoon February 15th I'm especially at home. Don't be scared to come. And why not bring your half arsed butler with you.

Burning the other replies in the drawing room fire I carefully refolded this letter in its envelope and put it in my wallet. Carrying it with me and rereading it nearly a dozen times. Amazed that anybody but Laura could ever stimulate my interest again. My presently quarter arsed butler Austin, who now spent an hour polishing his teeth and grinning in every mirror, was increasingly more desperate about his acting career. Even came in bringing my breakfast dressed as an Arab, sending a jolt of unneeded apoplexy through me as I woke. He needed two hours off to go to an audition that morning as doorman at a new Moorish nightclub. But after another day of melancholia I certainly didn't need being frightened to death.

'I say Austin, I'm planning to soon hold an audition.'

'For what sir.'

'A bloody damn new butler.'

Long faced Austin didn't think my suggestion was at all funny. Complained to his aunt and then arrived next day in a ten gallon hat, leather chaps, cowboy boots and spurs and then without asking for two hours off, disappeared for the rest of the day carrying off my De Alfonce Tennis case as a prop. But I finally cheered a little at the Game Club, winning third place in the metropolitan sabre championships. And was even asked for my autograph by a small but attractively shaped lady in the audience. And now more out of devilment than despair, my optimism somewhat renewed, I dared order a limousine for the coming Saturday.

Although another blizzard was again predicted, the roads and sky were clear. Austin, who even failed his audition as a cowboy prop outside a steak restaurant, was nearly glad to still have a job making me an egg sandwich or two, and magnanimously polished an apple with which to escort me down to the waiting limousine. Just as I was going out the door, my old girlfriend Sue rang. Said she was that day flying in from Palm Beach, having lost her month's alimony on the horses.

'Those god damn things J.P. just like men, can't be trusted. Not only lost my shift and brassière but also have had to eat my principle not to have free dinners with repulsive guys.'

Speaking of brassières, Laura's was now nearly permanently tied around my thigh. By way of a weak excuse I explained to Sue I was on my way to an Arab horse auction in Connecticut, which in fact was partially true. I must say it felt quite good to be on the street, wondering what the hell I was to be confronted with up in the sticks. As Austin watched, my chauffeur Burt saluted and even placed a warm rug over my knees. I even thought my half arsed butler actor was mildly jealous. Burt turned out to be a reformed alcoholic, for that day anyway.

'Drink anything I could get my hands on.'

Up the Bronx River Parkway I heard he had to stop being a waiter because he couldn't stop polishing off the unlimited free booze he stole. His life story summed up, was, that in each succeeding binge, the blank number of days when he didn't know where he was, grew longer. He certainly was no expert map reader, and we early abandoned looking for the Arab horse auction. Then Burt got us lost in a god forsaken neck of the woods, till we stopped to ask directions to Hawthorne Manse. And miracle of miracles it seemed we were as the crow flew, only a mile or two away. Burt offering the local man for this welcome news, a friendly cigarette out of the window.

'Do you smoke.'

'Nope. Ain't never got that hot.'

There was no doubt at least that we were in a clear

thinking rural area. But as we continued down into a gorge, and through a thick pine forest, the narrowing road following along by the white frozen edges of a winding river, I distinctly began to lose my nerve. And more so, following the local's advice.

'You wouldn't want to get stuck up in them parts. With the snow coming tonight.'

We turned right up a steep winding hill, with not a sign of habitation anywhere. Driving now, wheels skidding, nearly three or more miles on this bumpy narrow land through the woods, past a waterfall and a hauntingly white iced over lake. I was actually pressing my hand reassuringly on Laura's brassiere knotted under my trousers around my thigh. Then higher again where at a fork in the road there appeared a sign, its letters made of cats eyes.

'Hawthorne Manse'
Strictly Private

We entered and passed beneath a strange masonry arch flanked by enormous stone turreted gate lodges. And behind us a phalanx of large speared iron bars seemed to rise up from nowhere and close the road rearwards. I swallowed saliva. And Burt ducked as a Great Horned owl suddenly swooped down out of a tree. With its immense wide wings flapping, it flew low ahead of us over the bumpy gravel drive. The huge bird finally disappearing again into the woods as we came into a snow covered clearing. Two large hawthorn trees standing before a gabled, gothic, cut stone deceptively large cottage, fronted with a long verandah. There was something strangely familiar about the building as if I'd been there before but I knew I never had.

Burt stopped the car between two piles of snow at the front porch, rushing to open my door for me to get out. It was rapidly growing dark. Ominous black snow clouds piling up above the tree tops on the north horizon. The squawk of a bluejay coming through the crystal cold air. All made me shiver. A large gothic window over the verandah porch. This indeed was one hell of a very private and most extremely elegant mental institution. And somehow in this sylvan silent setting, one knew one was being stared at from somewhere.

'Is this the place sir.'

'I think so, Burt.'

Something I rarely do is to use someone's Christian name without knowing them for at least five years. But one felt one needed now a quick nearby friend. While looking back over both my shoulders I nervously went up on the porch and crossed to the door to press a black bell button. Ready to run in case a nutty inmate or grizzly bear any second came charging at us out of the woods. No sound inside and I was about to raise my finger to the bell again, when suddenly glancing down I saw in front of me, inside the curtained glass of the door, and in large childish and difficult to read letters, a sign.

J.P. you hard up snob
Are you
Ready for another trouncing on the Bangokok Court
Ha ha it's
Laura

I somehow couldn't believe the words. Cringing at first in embarrassment and then my lips breaking into a helpless smile. Followed by a long groan of relief. Now I remembered this house. From a photograph in the room full of the 'Fourteenth's' memorabilia in which his mother in tennis costume stood on this porch. And Burt behind me shouted.

'Anybody home sir.'

'Not that I can see.'

While Burt jumped up and down on his toes and clapped

his hands in the brisk cold, I peered in a window of an anteroom and caught sight of a lace covered dining room table set for tea. Still no answer came to my bell pushing, knocking or turning the handle of the locked door. And instead of explosive joy, a sickly desperate feeling of disappointment rose up from my toes and seeped through my whole being. Then I turned around. To a thunderous bark. A massive shaggy grey Irish wolfhound loomingly silhouetted against the snow. And by his barking brogue, I recognized Clare's dog I'd heard aboard ship. Burt was standing with his black gloved hands raised high in the air and a man in a red plaid woodsman's shirt, a peaked railman's cap on his head, was squinting his eyes over the twin barrels of a shotgun, which was now swivelling round to point directly at me.

'Just hold it right there a minute please.'

'I'm J.P., I actually am. And I understand this is Hawthorne Manse.'

'I reckoned it was who you might be. I'm Zeke. Excuse the firearm. It's kinda lonely up here and you kinda have to be careful of strangers. Lady Laura was expected yesterday to land in Armonk. And haven't heard since. Reckon she must have changed her plans. But you're welcome to go in where it's warm.'

A clock tower tolled four and a glockenspiel played 'Annie Laurie'. It appeared that Hawthorne Manse and its out buildings and gate lodges were isolated high on a cleared summit of a mountainous island surrounded by thick inpenetrable forest, which by summer, was a copperhead snake infested swamp, and stone cliffs and outcroppings allowed the only approach on the narrow lane over which we had come. A little distance off in the trees there was what looked like stables and garages. And Zeke, from a large bundle of keys, now chose two, to open two different locks, to allow us to enter this exquisite gothic building, into a large vestibule full of canes, boots and polo mallets.

Further through large glass doors, a vast drawing room asprawl with immense sofas, high backed chairs, two massive refectory tables and four chimney pieces. Over one of which was an enormous painting of a greyhound attacking a stag in a sombre stormy landscape.

'Get you folk a drink maybe.'

Burt was licking his lips and even though I knew I needed a drink more badly than he did, I asked Zeke for a cup of tea and ventured in the direction of an opening to another sitting room. Its interior dark and austere and in the corners of which was statuary set in carved gothic niches. My eyes getting used to the faint light, I could see against one wall a great glass case in which a large model of a yacht sat resplendent in its every astonishing tiny definition. And on a brass plate its name, 'Hiyathere'.

Zeke brought me tea and Burt a beer, then beckoned me to a set of double curtained French doors opening off the drawing room. Unlocking one, he ushered me to step through. From a balcony where one stood, one was astonished to look down at this awesome sight. There below, roofed under a vast glass domed arena held high by baroque pavilions, two Bangokok courts side by side, ready for play. A crimson ribbon tape, stretched between the mast uprights, suspending the purple nets. In this large chamber, eerie music, a female soprano voice accompanied by an organ was echoing Charles Gounod's 'Ave Maria'. I stood there, tears welling in my eyes knowing somehow for certain that Laura was not to appear.

The snow already falling, we hurried to beat the approaching storm back to New York. Burt's speech on two beers, slightly slurred. And we almost killed a deer as it jumped across our path. Our car lights sweeping through the woods catching the eyes of two more. I had the uncomfortable feeling of still being watched. Opening the window to peek ahead as we approached the gate lodges, the speared iron bars under the arch, lowering. Then I suddenly saw perched up on a turret of this strange structure, the Great Horned owl, its fearless evil eyes watching in our light beam. And only feet away, on a balcony turret, bundled in scarves and coats and now hurriedly stepping inside, the faces of the Commodore, his oriental friend and the French professor.

As we reached the bottom of the hill I took out the letter once more and reread it in the map light. Not only was the lady clearly a literary genius, of beauty, riches, charm, but with such spectres looming about in her life, I was certain she must also be the strange heroine member of some secret intelligence service.

On our way back to the city we drove through the village of Armonk, past a pretty white church, and later the small airport where Laura was to have landed. All one could think of, watching the houses in the trees, alone in this night, was that, together, in one of them with her, I would be content. During that last entire evening, not daring to kiss her. She had even held open her arms to me once and said, didn't I think that at least she deserved from me a hug. And I knew, had I enclosed and squeezed my own arms around her, I simply would never ever have let her go.

The storm behind us as we returned down through the valley of the Bronx River to New York, I steeled myself, to prepare for the evening of loneliness ahead. Looking up at the thousands of bright yellow lit windows in the palisades of buildings enclosing Central Park. Hoping someone might still be on the badminton courts or even playing basketball. But only one member was left in the Great Room of the Game Club, the custodian already switching off the lights, and not noticing this elderly gentleman, who chewing on an unlit cigar and watching himself in a large wall mirror, was cantering on the mechanical horse.

Suddenly as I stood in the shadows watching, the mirror came crashing down off the wall. And I swear, shying the mechanical horse into bucking. Throwing the old gent tumbling in a somersault to the exercise mat, his unlit cigar, smashing all over his face.

By the time I had rushed to his aid, the tough old bird, ninety three years old, had already picked himself up. Although I'd seen him come and go for nearly a quarter of a century, amazingly we met only now for the first time and shook hands. I expressed astonishment at his physical fitness which enabled him unscathed to take such a fall.

'Raw carrots, and Bangokok ball my boy, and the odd good woman firmly dealt with, that's what does it. And now that court sits there unused. Damned disgrace. And please call me Ed.'

The card room empty as I passed, and it was eight p.m. by the chiming grandfather clock in the Game Club library. To keep my spirits up, I was planning a hamburger, salad and beer with apple pie à la mode and coffee in the Club dining room. Hoping then to find a partner for three cushioned billiards, before setting off up Fifth Avenue home to watch some boxing and basketball on television. I hadn't for two whole days seen the newspaper. And sat now to read that stocks were up sharply as traders exuded growing confidence. The Dow Jones Industrial Average finished over eight hundred. The dollar was mixed and gold was up in tranquil trading. Murders normal, at a steady eighteen a week. A gentle, gifted and compassionate young man stabbed to death on a subway train. Lieutenant Alias clearly kept busy. And a blizzard warning on the weather page, that temperatures would be falling to ten below freezing in the night.

I crossed my legs to read an article about the supplementing of two tunnels already bringing nearly one and a half billion gallons of water flowing daily into the city. With plans to build another boring twenty four feet in diameter, six hundred feet beneath the Bronx and into the solid rock of Manhattan. I was about to switch off the reading lamp hovering above my chair, when my eye saw at the bottom of the newspaper page I'd just been reading, a column headed 'Around the Nation', and a small headline:

ROLLS ROYCE PLUNGES INTO GRAND CANYON

Three as yet unidentified people at noon today, believed a man and two women, were seen wearing strange clothing in a Rolls Royce which careered off the road crossing open desert out of control, and breaking through a fence scattering tourists, smashed a barrier at a viewing platform, to plunge down the steep rough terrain into an inaccessible part of the Canyon. The state police authorities said they were already making their way to the vehicle and should reach it before nightfall.

The heaving of my breath made me stand up. To walk in the hushed emptiness of the room to the window. The wind howling outside, driving swirling thicknesses of snow in a great white veil sweeping down over the park. Blue bolts of lightning striking from the sky. Traffic slowing stopped in the streets. The glass of the Game Club library shaking with the claps of thunder. Cars far below, white little heaps abandoned. People staring from their windows. Dark tiny figures struggling into the wind. Under the pearly blanket, the noises of the city muffled to alabaster silence.

Upon this evening, out into this snowy sight to stare. The heat hissing hot in the Game Club pipes. The thought of Laura in one's arms. Blessed pause from pain back on that great ship, its throbbing engines ploughing the lonely ocean towards this land. My hand in her hand. My body in hers while she slowly fell into sleep. Her fingers loosening her grip as in death and dying. Her caress ebbing from mine, notch by notch, touch by touch. The top of her shoulder alight from the moonlit porthole in the cabin darkness. The grey strange rare pearls around her neck. Her hair, black soft strands across the white velvet curvatures of her ear. Her long silken legs locked upon my haunches by her magnificent sinewed feet. For those tiny seconds.

To drink
From her mouths
And lay
Softly by
Her soul

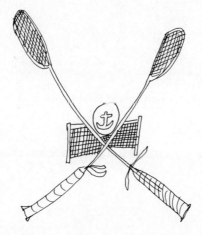

# ACCOUTREMENTS

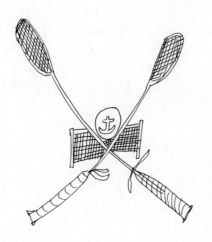

## The Playing Court

As this will prove to be where you will spend some of the most enjoyable moments of your life, every care should be given to the court's condition, and where largesse provides, its elegance and atmospherics. Any flat surface that does not unduly absorb the ball's bounce is suitable for play provided it is of firm foundation, and non skid. It may be of hard wood, maple, teak or oak or material similar, and may include steel deck for on board ship play. The floor colour is dark moss green and except for the Enceinte De Alfonce Spectator court, the side and stern bulkheads surrounds, are light moss green thus providing a clear definition in flight of the primrose coloured ball.

## The Net

Dark purple in colour, the net should be of the best cotton string material of three quarter inch net openings. The binding tape at the top suspending the net should be one and a half inches broad, and bright crimson in colour to recall the original ribbon used by the first oarsmen. The top edge of the net, two feet four inches high, is drawn rigidly straight across the court, a white satin ribbon tie string at mid top net anchoring the net to the brass memorial plate.

## Net Mast

Except in Enceinte De Alfonce where the net is wall anchored, the post supporting the net may be made of any strong metal or plastic. For purists of the game and elegant circumstances providing, polished walnut, rose or teak wood is to be preferred. And for ultra purists, polished ebony.

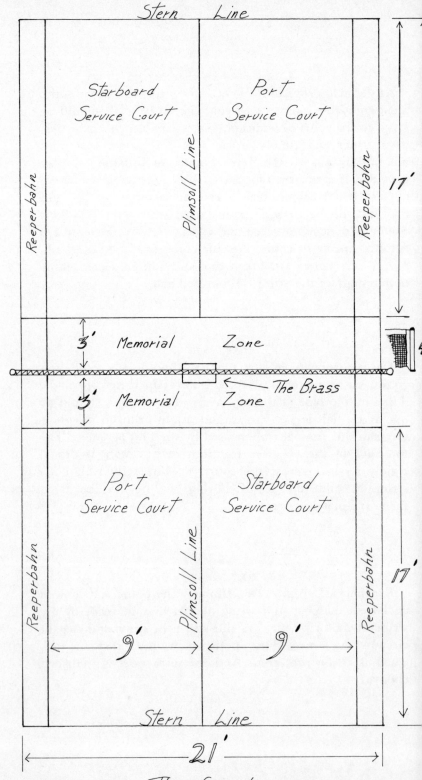

The Court

ACCOUTREMENTS

## The Glass

Except for vaulted ceiling play dealt with under the chapter, 'Adaptations', the Glass is that area above the court forming the ceiling and so named following its use and design on the ship 'Hiyathere'. This surface may be of any flat ceiling material and, except for the Enceinte Spectator Court, is cerulean blue in colour, giving an outdoor quality to indoor confines, as well as being effective as an overhead ball background. One of the most exciting aspects of De Alfonce is the Le Ricochet play off the Glass into your opponent's court from above. The optimum and match play height of the Glass is thirteen feet. But it may be varied based on the perpendicular room needed for the tallest player to adequately swing his racquet while fully extended on tip toe, always providing such player is not capable of executing a jump smash twirl shot, which brings him into collision with the ceiling.

## The Brass

The memorial brass at the net centre of the court, to which the mid net tie string is attached, is inlaid mid memorial zone and is referred to as the Brass. It extends six inches either side of the net and is fourteen inches wide. Owners should not engrave the Brass with their own escutcheon but purists, upon application to the World De Alfonce Tennis Association, may emplace there the Association's emblem. The Brass is out of play at all times for both ball and the feet of players.

## The Bulkheads

These are the adjoining side and end walls of the court. And where they are not close confined, as in Enceinte De Alfonce, such bulkheads are optional in play, the ball striking the bulkhead, and bouncing into court. End walls are referred to as the Stern Bulkheads.

## MEMORIAL ZONE

This area extending three feet broad either side of the net, recalls the disappearance of the original 'thirteen'. The section is crimson in colour and is out of play in volleying for serve and in service.

## PLIMSOLL LINE

This is the line dividing the court down its centre and separating the Port service court, from the Starboard.

## THE REEPERBAHN

The Reeperbahn, so named after the strange sightings of 'Hiyathere' passengers on the notorious Hamburg boulevard, extends one and a half feet broad the full length both sides of the court and its use is for doubles play.

## FIFTH AND MADISON

Present only in Enceinte De Alfonce and so named following the many lonely nightly walks the Honourable Founder, bereft of Laura, took and has taken along both these New York City avenues. These foot wide areas are out of play and extend the court length between the Reeperbahn and Bulkhead.

## LINE MARKINGS

Line markings are white and one and a half inches wide. The line at the ends of court is referred to as the Stern line.

## COURT SURROUNDS

This area in De Alfonce play, ideally should allow space for the return of deep service to the Stern line as well as cross court drives and finessing at the net, the latter a speciality of De Alfonce play. Where there are no close adjoining side and Stern Bulkheads as in Enceinte De Alfonce play, open space should extend six feet either side of the Reeperbahns and ten feet beyond the Stern lines. An arena sixty feet by thirty three, therefore providing optimum minimum dimensions for the location of the playing court and its surrounds.

## THE SERVICE COURT

In Enceinte De Alfonce, the ball in service, must land bene in this area which extends nine feet in width between the Plimsoll line and Reeperbahn and fifteen feet in length between the Memorial Zone to two feet in from the Stern line. In open De Alfonce the service court extends seventeen feet from the Memorial Zone to the Stern line.

## THE RACQUET

The feather light racquet must, irrespective of the material of its manufacture, not weigh less than four ounces or more than four and a half ounces. The hand grip extends for a full seven and one quarter inches which allows for choking up leverage grip upon the racquet for volley and finessing play at the net. The crimson satin bow at the top of the hand grip is commemorative of the tie string on the first hand gloves used by the original oarsmen. The colour purple is optional for purists. The bow extends three inches and is three eighths of an inch wide and should freely flutter. The blade of the racquet contains twenty three strings across and twenty three strings down. The top of the racquet is flattened but retains the slightest curvature, allowing for service of the Nurt or Floater ball. Perfection of this skilled and rarely returnable service shot is fully dealt with under its later appropriate heading.

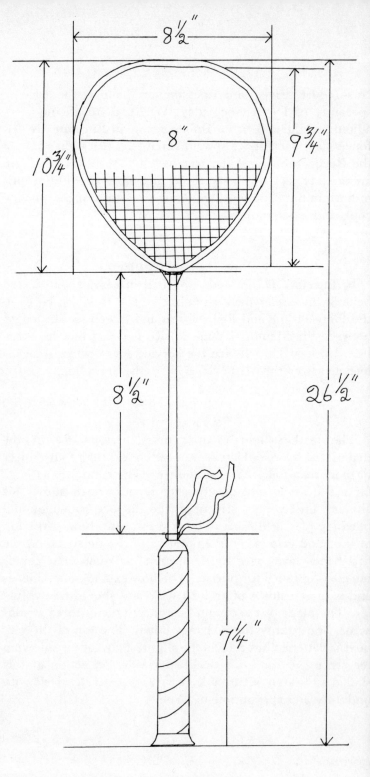

The Racquet

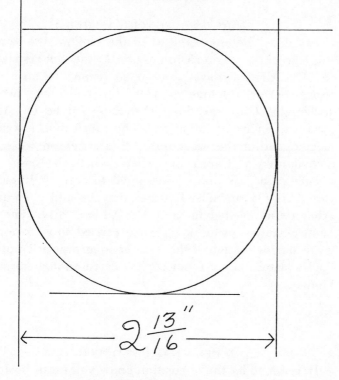

## The Ball

The above dimension in diameter and weighing less than 6 grams, the ball is made of a solid net mesh of resilient foam plastic, its rough outer surface although seeming a contradiction in aerodynamics, provides reduced wind resistance in its projectory as well as air friction in spin and slice shots, enabling the ball to achieve pronounced curvature in flight. Free dropped from a height of six feet the quotient of aeroelastic divergence in the ball's bounce should achieve a minimum bounce of two feet and a maximum of two feet two inches high. The official approved ball will have upon it imprinted the emblem marking of The World De Alfonce Tennis Association and such authenticated ball is required use in all match play establishing national or international player ranking.

## THE DE ALFONCE VASCULUM

Based on the one bequeathed the Honourable Founder, this leather bound music box case is the pièce de résistance of the De Alfonce player, and is so named because of the 'Fourteenth's' lifelong passion for collecting botanical specimens. Only the finest materials will be De Alfonce approved in its manufacture. The music box is centrally located within the vasculum and is synchronized to play Tchaikovsky's 'Capriccio Italien' when the case top is opened. The vasculum is designed to carry four racquets and a supply of balls. Pouches may be added to include other items needed in your De Alfonce play. The brass name plate is upside down when carried so as to force an awkward inclination of the head upon anyone attempting to read a name they are not sophisticated enough to already know.

## APPAREL
## AND PERSONAL PARAPHERNALIA

In order to let the opposition know you mean business it is essential the correct dress be always worn on court. To the lay observer this may seem a superficial matter but in the conduct of De Alfonce whose adherents, some to the point of mild mania, are obsessive about their sport, any variation from proper apparel disgruntles and distracts from the intense pleasure a veteran player has grown accustomed to expect from his game. As an opponent you may assume this to be to your advantage, but be warned. It invariably makes your matured player implacably and dedicatedly strategize against you. In fact he will verily exert every overt and sly effort to make you look a total chump, again and again executing his most skilled Nurt and net cross court passing shots, leaving you singularly and repeatedly lax in your tracks, and dismally conscious the floor has been immaculately wiped with your person.

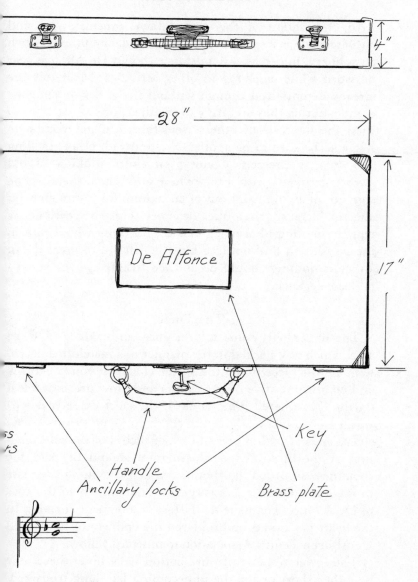

The De Alfonce Vasculum
and music box

In observation of this same above consideration, and although one is aware of the strong tendency to exert such a snobbery, under no circumstance should De Alfonce gear be worn while engaging in other activities. Most folk are already demoralized enough without the antics of someone demonstrating they are privy to an elite sport.

In the interests of others' sensibilities if not your own hygiene, be sure to be spotlessly laundered, clean smelling and smartly pressed. Coming on court stinking of old sweaty garments with a tatter here and a hole there, is the sign not of an old hand but of an unmindful commoner. Of course blatantly baroque designer created costume is equally inviting of askance looks. And those who aspire to the garish will find nothing but the fish eye to greet them. In short nothing should be allowed to infringe the court's tableau elegance.

### The Tunic

The upper part consists of a pure cotton navy blue tee shirt which is V necked in the manner of a matelote uniform with a cross piece filling the V, the colour of which is black and commemorative of the sailors and crew presumed lost on the 'Hiyathere'. The trunk of the shirt extends downwards to two inches above the cheek curve on the arse. The sleeve ends at within one and a half inches of the mid position of the bicep. Especial attention should be paid the roominess accorded the shoulder which should be adequate to accommodate the full service motion which in the case of De Alfonce Tennis is the fastest of any racquet sport. In the heart position is embroidered the emblem of the World De Alfonce Tennis Association in mustard yellow.

The lower tunic is of pure cotton navy blue, these may be either short or for the unbecoming leg, long trousered. Snug but not tight fitting across the arse area, the bottom end of the shorts should not extend more than one and a half inches above or below mid thigh. The garment may be discreetly pleated at the waist and a side split provided for full movement, allowing for the knee to be raised without hindrance to touch the shoulder. For men there should be an adequately disguised button fly for peeing. In the case of ladies the tunic may be designed in one piece. The shirt is always worn inside the shorts, and an umpire may stop play to so ensure.

## The Sock

It is essential to have this utterly vital garment comfortable in fitting and of a fully sweat absorbing fibre. The toe, foot and heel part of the sock should be so shaped not to lump and should extend on the ankle and leg up to but not beyond the calf muscle. The elastic quality of the sock should be sufficient for the sock to remain pulled up. Bending down during doubles play to hoist up your footwear can get you clubbed into insensibility when you stand up again into the trajectory of your partner's racquet.

In the case of the form fitting sock shaped to the rake of the toes, socks should be embroidered with the letters 'S' for the starboard foot and 'P' for the port foot. The W.D.T.A. emblem, adorns at three inches above the ankle bone. Two pairs of socks, one worn over the other allows for a cushioning effect and adequate absorption of moisture from perspiration, which helps to keep athlete's foot in check, a subject more fully dealt with under that later heading.

## The Shoe

The W.D.T.A. make every effort to exert rigid standards in according official approval of their shoes. To adhere to the court surface in the rapid and sometimes violent change of play position, a full non skid sole is essential. As is cushioning adequate to aborb the foot concussion when landing from a jump twirl smash shot. The upper fabric of the shoe should be of a suitably ventilated leather insulated with soft cushioning ridges around the ankle and heel and may be entirely black or white, but should not be decorated with stripes or other embellishments. Remember in the fitting of your shoe that it should provide for two sock thicknesses.

Footwear, not surprisingly, as it is often the most expensive part of your regalia, is the first thing your opponent will notice about you on court. Elegance in the matter is a distinct plus. Old ragged, clapped out, flap and slap prone sneakers worn smooth on the sole and on which you slide to fracture your arse, if you haven't already tripped and broken your skull, or which are likely to go flying from the foot, have no place on the De Alfonce court. The tie bow of laces should be short and not act as lassos. Except of course for laughs during a celebratory post championship champagne circus event, which is fully dealt with under the later heading, The De Alfonce Ball.

### Sweat Bands

For tournament match play, these should be pure cotton and in hue, navy blue. Care being taken that they are snug but not too tight to the point of restricting the blood flow in the wrists. There is nothing worse than an ashen handed player either dropping his racquet or sending it twirling boomerang fashion as an airborne scimitar across court.

When the sweat band is worn around the head in the manner of the American Indian it is referred to as a 'Lord Charles'. As adornment, the sweat band, although insignificant in size, is an article of wear which can be spectacular in effect. And for ordinary play colour may be optional. Tints such as pink being appropriate to ladies. Crimson to gents. But in this realm of De Alfonce Tennis accoutrement a designer may adorn you to the heights of his or your fancy.

## Medical Wear and Appliances

De Alfonce being one of the few racquet sports permitting infirm play, it is not done to jeopardize your safety or that of others. Never appear on court as if you ought to be in hospital. Although it is permissible for you to take all remedy and precaution with medical fitments, these in the case of prosthesis should be checked by a medical engineer for stress factors, loose screws, springs, swivels and metal fatigue in the privacy of your home or doctor's office and never at the venue of play. It is considerably off putting where a gent is conspicuously having his knee screws tightened prior to a match in full view of spectators and of his adversary. And then goes limping on court and trounces this able limbed opponent ragged. Similarly make sure that moving parts are well oiled to avoid squeaks. In the case of trusses and the like, it is disconcerting, to put it mildly, when your own or an opponent's entrails suddenly fall out of their rigging.

## Underfittings for Ladies

To avoid risking gross embarrassments, flimsiness is totally out of place here. It is of signal priority that the bosoms, in the case of the generously endowed woman, have full and firm enclosure. The larger variety of these glands can not only hamper her play but also lead to a major focus of attention on court. Along with the self consciousness a player herself may suffer, this area of the female anatomy also intrudes upon the concentration of male and indeed some female players, as the Honourable Founder is most acutely aware in the case of the lissome Laura. Nor to be overlooked is the fact that some hormone hyped spectators, in whom bouncing bosoms produces an explosive emotion, may be provoked from their seats to interfere with play.

Although silk is an elegant comfortable fabric, its tendency to slide against the skin does not recommend its wear, and the bra should therefore be of seamless cotton which can provide a reliable skid free cradle for the bosoms. Such garment should be well elasticated and strong to stay in place during the vigorous raising and swinging of the arms at the shoulder during service and especially in executing the jump twirl smash.

Despite the engineering difficulties of appendage enclosure, there is no physical reason why a lady should not remain feminine and discreet bows are not out of place. However these, on the bra, should be located downside between the cleavage, as nothing is more aesthetically displeasing than nobbles and bumps under snug fitting garments.

In extreme cases of largeness or nipple oversize, which latter the seamless bra tends to accentuate, two well designed bras may be worn, one over the other. These reduce both undue bosom bounce and the attention nipples always attract by their prominence.

Although it may gently suggest such curvature, lower underwear fittings should not show up unduly the pelvic and adrectal areas. Silk may be worn and at the bifurcation opaqueness is a must. Frills and furbelows are best left to your designer.

### Underfittings for Gentlemen

None is more vital than the euphemistically referred to athletic supporter, or as it is more commonly known, the jock strap. Couching the penis and testicles, this item of protection should never be worn in a manner that sees you strutting about as a male ballet star in full plumage.

This rigging should be of a cotton fabric, stout enough to be fully cut proof and to cushion a stray racquet blow, the edge of which, wielded at full stretch, is capable of shortening the penis or desacing the gonads, if indeed it doesn't remove all three items entirely. The supporting straps holding the protective cup over the business area of the privates should be broad and elasticated enough not to rope, fold or ruckle. However, as strong and snugly fitting as the jock strap should be, it should allow for sudden and unpremeditated erection. Such expansive predicament being highly painful and hampering as the Honourable Founder knows from play with the ebullient Laura. If you are overlarge in the first place, do take the trouble to obtain a tailor made garment. Loose jangling pudenda commits a true felony in taste on court.

Of all under items this is the one which frequent laundering should not overlook. In the same context, the straggly stray ends of this garment left hanging loose out from under your shorts, fluttering, and god forbid, soiled, can bring, if not a thunderclap of revulsion then at least a never forgotten shudder of distaste. Ragged remnants of this underfitting displayed is the extreme of inappropriate dress on court.

## Warm Up Gear

This should be of natural fibre, and except for the small black memorial ball located under the left breast and upon which shall be embroidered the mustard yellow emblem of the W.D.T.A., this two piece garment should be absolutely snow white. In tournament match play it presents a dramatic moment, especially on the Enceinte see through Spectator Court, when the warm up suit is removed. The loose fitting jacket should have a neck flap high enough to cover the jugular vein and be zippered down the front. Good quality long lasting elastic on the belt of the trouser part is essential. Zippers on the leg sides should allow easy exit and entrance of your playing shoe.

## Head Covering

The official permitted bonnet is a white cap with visor which should be of the best linen or cotton material and may be worn by both ladies and gentlemen.

Such is referred to as the 'bonnet' in commemoration of

Lord Charles' proclivity for such wear. However, players are not encouraged to emulate that pissing peer by throwing mid court tantrums in which such headgear, being flung to the floor, is then jumped and trampled upon and kicked to remnants with both feet.

## The Handkerchief

One might expostulate straight off to divest of the ephemeral. But provided it is sweat absorbent such above cloth is an essential tool on court. And two are necessary. While one is used for nose blowing, the other serves for perspiration and racquet handle and other wipings. Purists may differentiate their hankies by the colours navy blue and mustard yellow.

A third sterilized hanky may be kept in reserve in the case of head collision or racquet injury. Such cloth applied to the site, can temporarily staunch all but the most heavily pumping artery wounds. But do not use a hanky into which your nose has already been blown for this emergency purpose.

As this is an item not part of the official De Alfonce Tennis costume, colour is at your discretion. But it should not lead to capriciousness nor to the magician's variety, where the court joker type strings out of his pocket a dozen multi coloured rags. Nor should chaps be seen dragging out hankies big enough for a tent or parachute. All the above same basic rules apply to neckwear involving scarfs, cravats or chokers.

## Note for Designers

Within the necessarily strict framework of the code of dress for De Alfonce Tennis which evolved from the long and albeit mysterious history of the game, there still remains considerable room for innovative design. The W.D.T.A. does of course allow for the greatest latitude in ladies' court costume. This however should never be instrusive in terms of the overall costume or violate the fabrics specified. Adornments such as lace, frills, bustles and bows etc. should never be garish, or insinuating, or most importantly, interfere with free and easy body movement on court. Upon application, the W.D.T.A. is always glad to consider giving its official approval and to permit use of the De Alfonce Tennis emblem to a designer and to allow license to design De Alfonce wear within the above scope, and in special cases and countries, to do so on an exclusive basis.

## TROPHIES

With words unboasting, nothing untoward here must dismay. And being mindful of the tradition, fortitudes and character associated with the sport of De Alfonce Tennis, all honours accorded in its pursuit must be tasteful and avoid any indecent or garish motif or curvature. Precious metals are in order but gems should not be used.

Provided it is prior approved by the W.D.T.A., and carries the emblem, a trophy may exist in the form of any useful ornament, placard, testimonial, citation, plate, cup or glass. However most suitable of all is a small replica of crossed De Alfonce racquets on a ball, shafts En Croissant, in the form of a solid silver pin, upon which is engraved on the reverse, the details of the win. With the De Alfonce Tennis emblem outermost on each blade, this is a most suitable decoration for ladies, especially at the annual De Alfonce ball.

Because most of its historical antecedents were vastly rich and its present day adherents are at least financially mildly comfortable, under no circumstances, is the game of De Alfonce Tennis to be played for monetary reward. The personally felt esteem triumphing at De Alfonce should be everything looked for in executing excellence at play. And only in the most extreme extenuating circumstances approved of as warranted by the W.D.T.A., may large bonanza winnings be permitted to befall De Alfonce players, who in such case will covenant two and a half percent of such gross winnings to be used at the discretion of the Honourable Founder in the celebration and furtherance of the sport.

### THE EMBLEM

The emblem is that of the World De Alfonce Tennis Association and is the official stamp of the Association which alone may authorize the manufacture of and authenticate the ball, racquet, net, court, gear, materials and colours as those approved by the technical committee of the Association and which are required to be used in all match play from which the official world rankings of players shall derive.

The emblem symbolically commemorates both the ancient and modern associations of the game. The left hand and the dangling tie string attributes to the original doe skin glove first worn in the playing of Bangokok. The sim-

ple circle recalls the ball beneath which is the diamond
tipped assassin's bullet. The anchor is a facsimile of one of
the twin bow anchors of the motor ship 'Hiyathere'. Tre-
decim being the Latin for the number thirteen, recalling
the eccentric stalwarts of that fated voyage, not to mention
Friday the thirteenth upon which date saw the demise of
the 'Fourteenth' whose legacy gave birth to the first De
Alfonce Tennis racquet and ball.

## THE EDIFICE

Housed in its own detached structure, be it Gothic, Eliza-
bethan or just plain old ordinary Cape Cod, its presence
can not only enhance your squirearchical pretensions and
athletic prowess, but also the property value of your estate.
And in this, the ultra de luxe version of the De Alfonce
court, you can really go all out to express yourself architec-
turally, secure in the promise that the result will avail you
of life long fitness and pleasure.

Although with paper, rulers and pencils easy to hand, you
may do your own early sketches, it is of course wisest to
conjure up the actual elevations and choice of building
material, in the presence of, and in consultation with your
architect, as only he or she can expect to cope with the
myriad of plumbing, heating and general engineering miracles necessary to equip this elaborate plant. And do make
sure your architect has a smilingly cheerful sympathetic and
enthusiastic vision for such matters. In the absence of such
professional help and advice, basic plans may be obtained
at a reasonable fee from the De Alfonce Institute.

For those grandees of the sport there is an unquestionable
excitement about your Enceinte court being actually inside
and part of your residence. Making it a sublimely pleasing
matter to arise up out of your sofa from your repartee with
an invited guest, and in a few steps find yourselves light-
hearted with anticipation in the hormone inspiring confines

of this life ennobling arena. Provided they do not affront
official De Alfonce accoutrements, there is no reason why
the rare and fine materials used by your architect in the rest
of your dwelling cannot find their way to embellishing the
confines of your court, thus making it, despite its necessary
utilitarian aspects, a place of utter awe inspiring grandeur.
Not only can the interior be spectacular in its use of wall
and ceiling glass inlays for light but also, in the case of an
Enceinte see through court, the simple spatial splendour
created by bulkhead, floor and ceiling surfaces, can, in their
rectilinear perfections make even strong stern persons
brought within such sanctuary, openly weep.

Nor should a warmer domestic intimacy be overlooked.
For your court, when not in use for play, may convert to a
sumptuous chandelier lit ballroom or on less formal occasions, to provide for plenty of stomping amid the straw and
pumpkins when holding your barn dance. A dais is easily
erected at one end for your orchestra or country and western band. But do place a protective cordon around The
Brass so that this memorial is not trod upon.

Essentially the building structure housing the court
should incorporate a terraced solarium and the accoutrements of a sauna, spout shower, whirlpool bath, dressing
rooms and swimming pool. A cloakroom vestibule area
should be attached to accommodate the reception of guest
players. A pantry area is also required so that when
conducting your entertainments or giving large parties, or
gala dinners, service may easily flow from your domestic
kitchens which should adjoin the De Alfonce area. Warning, do not locate your champagne and wine cellars near
pool purification or heating equipment. And adequate closets to store balls, racquets and apparel, are a must, and
particularly as a safe place to keep your crystal chandelier
while removed during play.

For practical considerations, weight of water etcetera
your swimming pool should be located at or below ground

level, and beneath the area of the De Alfonce court. On the same level may also be located your spout showers, dressing room and sauna, access to which is made by elevator and also by spiral staircase. This latter cantilevered in stone, inside an adjoining tower can be spectacular indeed, not only giving entree to your residential floors, but also offsetting any overall rectangular tendency of the primary structure. And certainly not least, adds an edificial nobility to your entire estate. However, should you be a real risk taker, your pool may be structured over your De Alfonce court, with the pool's transparent bottom forming 'The Glass' ceiling enabling underwater swimmers above to view De Alfonce play below.

Sea and ocean coasts provide especially attractive architectural situations to be aesthetically exploited. On sheer cliff sides facing the sea, your pool and court walls may be, in the see through Enceinte manner, entirely of glass. Take care though that the glass used prevents you from being roasted on sunny days. Also in such appropriate climes, there may be located an additional outdoor pool, which in turn permits beach and sea bathing. In the chillier latitudes and for summer use, a terrace can be provided alongside your De Alfonce edifice to overlook the outdoor pool and be availed of for al fresco dining. Your architect should also be conscious of having either indoor or outdoor, an area for solitary De Alfonce practice. Like masturbation it does have its pleasures.

Do not hesitate to castellate your tower and provide a mast top, from which to fly your De Alfonce flag. Although assuming such baronial prerogatives is not always certain to impress guests, who may know of your less than grand pedigree, it will nevertheless be an appropriate touch when you gather the more superficial of your people to attend your small recital or to perform at amateur theatricals within the confines of your De Alfonce court, temporarily adapted for the purpose. Remember everyone is going to want to see inside this structure, and there will be a premium on tickets for cultural gatherings. But please don't be tempted to start charging admission, unless it is for charitable purposes, when in such case the sums you may withhold, are exclusively used to defray your extremely high overhead expenses.

In choosing not to reside above your pool and De Alfonce court, any attic space existing may then serve for guest suites or for indulging your favourite hobby. But never adapt these for your butler, cook, maintenance man or other staff, in which to live, as they are liable to avail of the opportunity to become outstanding De Alfonce players and trounce you at your own game and with it lose their obedience and perhaps even become blatantly insolent.

An important concern, especially for those rich enough to build such previous edifice, is security. And providentially your pool walls reaching up through the further floor of your De Alfonce court, can provide a windowless wall expanse rising thirty or more feet from ground level, which presents to the outside world an unbreachable barrier not only in terms of pedestrian entry but also for bullets. Granite ashlar or four inch marble facings on thirteen inch reinforced concrete afford protection against most assaults provided smaller weapons than twenty millimetre cannon or armour piercing anti tank weapons are used against you. Further wall thicknesses however, with specially hardened steel implants are effective against such latter artillery.

In the special case of nuclear attack you will require further advices from an architect specializing in this protection, who can also provide you with ancillary purification devices and food and water storage space. But do beware, with such a big comfortable bastion against nuclear holocaust, you are bound to suffer the moral dilemma of neighbours not as well blessed, thronged on your lawns, tearfully begging on their knees to join you in a game of De Alfonce. But again, don't depend upon such non violent demonstration and best to consult with your architect for gun emplacements. Meanwhile, while the outside radiation subsidies, you may, in pursuing your De Alfonce regimen, maintain your immune system in combat readiness.


## THE DE ALFONCE ESTATE

Although one is not suggesting anything quite as elaborate or as invulnerable as the layout Laura took possession of from her loving cousin the 'Fourteenth', nevertheless for your ultra de luxe edifice you will need adequate acres. And why not really indulge yourself in this, which indeed may cost slightly less than your better quality private jet.

Although he may be no Capability Brown, starting from scratch with a suitable tract of land gives your landscape gardener a chance to show his paces. The site for the house should be raised and approached by an avenue of at least two hundred yards. This gives your arriving guests a dozen or so seconds to acquaint with your elevations if not to be in absolute awe of you. A pebbled drive helps add to an impeccable impression, with the sound of a tyre's hum over the gravel which, as it is cast up to tingle under the advancing vehicle's mudguards, reminds your visitors that indeed you are a grandee of sorts. But do flank your entrance gates with lodges to stop in their tracks by electric means, those who are only too eager to approach and become, as they freely quaff your De Alfonce champagne, grovelling claqueurs.

Within the vicinity of the edifice, a walled orchard is a nice sight upon which to open your bedroom window and also suits peacocks well. With money no object, and a few bulldozers at hand, provisions can be made for a jogging track which encircles a field for Polo, Soccer, Lacrosse, Cricket and Softball, all good ancillary sports to pursue when off the De Alfonce court. Surrounding areas of wood and pine forest help keep the air pure and provide a quiet

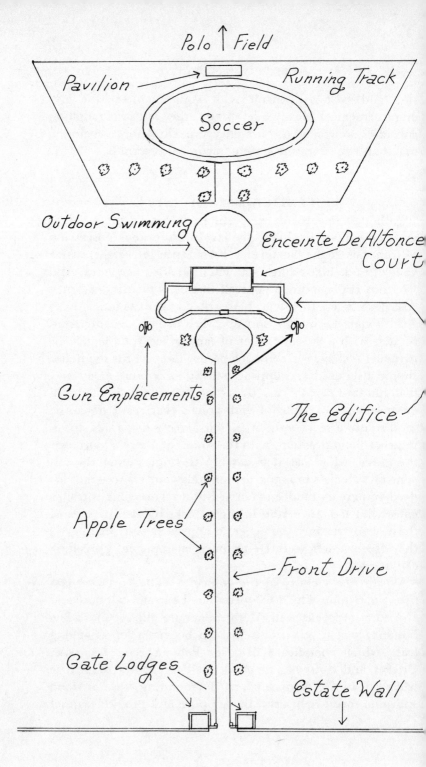

Polo ↑ Field

Pavilion

Running Track

Soccer

Outdoor Swimming

Enceinte De Alfonce Court

Gun Emplacements

The Edifice

Apple Trees

Front Drive

Gate Lodges

Estate Wall

DeAlfonce Estate

place to walk and meditate when you want a moment alone to cogitate your present imponderables, and to maintain your cheerful pessimism.

Plan too, a trout pond upon which your ducks, and swans may sail under the summer surrounds of its weeping willows. Do beware however, in such climes of the globe having them, of snapping turtles. There is nothing more dispiriting than when you have finished a strenuous De Alfonce game and you are, al fresco, gathered seated on the terrace with satisfied partners and guests, and the still calm of evening has settled on the day's events and your butler is busy serving the first glasses of champagne, and there, chuffed with the reassuring grandeur of it all, you point out your avian decorations afloat on your small body of water. Only to then silently gasp in horror as they suddenly, one by one, disappear below the surface, gobbled up by these rough carapaced hooked mouthed vicious amphibians greedily up for a morsel from the Stygian depths of your pond's muddy bottom.


## THE ENCEINTE DE ALFONCE SPECTATOR COURT

Erected for supreme Championship play in a suitable arena, this is essentially a plastic glass court which is entirely see-through from all directions. Illuminated and ventilated with the purest air to an ideal playing temperature, the court provides immaculate optimum conditions to players throughout a match. The court enclosure consists of see-through side and back bulkheads and see-through ceiling. In the hands of a gifted designer and lighting expert, it can provide one of the most beautifully spectacular of sporting venues possible, which, simply as an esoteric work of art and without its players, can be an exciting joy to contemplate. And in match play, within such court confines and setting, with the ball being finessed off the side and back bulkheads and the outwitting shots provided by

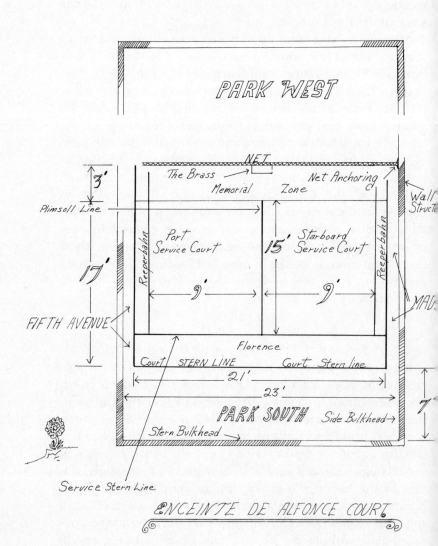

ENCEINTE DE ALFONCE COURT

ricochet play off the Glass, and with every stroke of the game intimately seen by spectators, Enceinte De Alfonce provides one of the most exotic and spectacular spectacles in the world of sport.

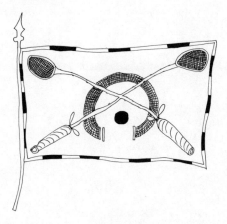

### THE FLAG

The thirteen border marks alternating with white, edge the De Alfonce flag and commemorate the 'Thirteen'. The black ball in the centre is in remembrance of the 'Fourteenth'. The flag background area enclosed by the border is cerulean blue and the racquet, net markings, and shark markings black, the teeth white and the shark mouth red. When a championship match is in progress, the flag with the shark mouths is displayed

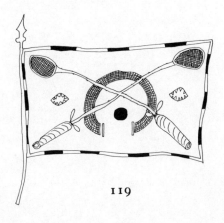

119

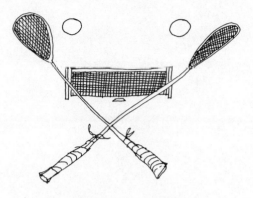

# RULES

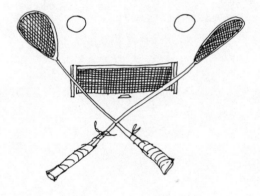

# ONE

Play consists of the ball being paddled by racquet over the net by one player on one side of the court to a player the other side of the net. The ball may be paddled by the receiver on the fly or after one bounce and thus returned. The point is won by the receiver when a ball is played out by a hitter, or he commits a culpa.

# TWO

All play for all tournaments and city, state, national or world ranking decided therefrom, shall only occur on the measured court as specified. Play may or may not include the Glass. Where the Glass is in play, its height, which shall not be lower than ten or higher than thirteen feet, shall apply uniformly to all players and play. In a large stadium, the Glass may consist above the court, of a transparent ceiling invisibly supported by transparent side and stern bulkheads the dimensions of which extend for doubles play. The rules of Glass play, apply to Bulkhead play. Where there is no Glass, the arena and court must then allow for an uninterrupted and unlimited height for lobbing. The term 'Culpa' is used to describe any fault in play, and the term 'Bene' to describe no fault.

# THREE

Apparel, Racquets and Balls shall in match play for rankings, accord to the given manual description and specifications. Immediately before match play commences there shall be a preamble on court of five seconds silence, the players standing motionless at the Plimsoll line adjoining the Memorial Zone. Although they may remain seated, spectators should be alerted by the umpire to similarly observe in silence. De Alfonce Tennis players among the audience will rise to attention, and will not hesitate to motion to those presuming this honour, for them to sit immediately down.


## Four

Warm up time for the players shall extend for three minutes. First service is awarded the winner of the volley for such service. The ball comes into volley play when it has been stroked four times over the court net. The counting of such strokes shall be cried out loud and distinct in the best coxswain manner by both players using the following appellation:

Semel

Bis

Ter

Quater

The player winning the volley may accept or decline to be first server. If he accepts service, he raises the ball above his shoulder in his opponent's sight.

Service is from any point behind the inside edge of the Stern line extending between the Reeperbahn on either side. The foot may be placed on but not inside the Stern line. Upon the ball being paddle stroked in a trajectory, the server's feet may then enter court for play. The Memorial Zone is out of play for service.

Service may be in any manner, the ball thrown up and struck or dropped and bounced outside the court and struck. However, only two throw ups or two bounces are permitted per service stroke and if, on the first throw up or bounce, the racquet has not come into contact with the ball, another throw up or bounce is allowed. If when the ball is thrown up or bounced for a second time and does not make contact with the racquet, it is a culpa.

First service failing to land in the opposite service court, a second service is permitted. A culpa on second service and the point is lost. The receiver may stand outside or in any part of his side of court except his feet may not enter upon or over the line of the Memorial Zone.

If the ball in service strikes the net and falls Bene into the receiver's service court, provided it does not land in the Memorial Zone, the ball is in play.

The service of the Nurt and Floater ball may result in the ball landing in the receiver's court and there proceed without a bounce along the floor. From the nature of this shot, such ball may be played by the receiver in any manner, provided the receiver's racquet does not come into contact with the floor, should the racquet do so, it is a culpa.

## FIVE

Except in Enceinte De Alfonce when side and stern Bulkheads and Glass are automatically in play, Bulkhead and play off the Glass must be firmly announced and agreed by players and umpire before the start of any match involving these surfaces. If no such announcement is made, they are to be ruled as out of play. In play, the ball in its trajectory may come into contact with any part of such surfaces on either side of the court, provided it falls Bene into the receiver's court.

## SIX

In match play for national and international ranking, new balls in the number of seven, replace used balls every seventh game. In other play new balls may replace those in play at the discretion of the umpire, or players. Any player may object to a ball and have the ball removed from court but only following the point in which he feels the offending ball has caused him to be aggrieved. However players should not lose sight of the fact that a worn gouged and pitted ball, seemingly on its last bounce, can provide an increased projectile curvature in spin shots.

## SEVEN

The ball is out of play when its circumference area contact is wholly made beyond a court line with no part of the ball touching such line. For a ball to be called a culpa it must land out of court. If the ball hits any part of a player standing in his court, other than his racquet, the ball is in play and such ball contact with the player shall count as the player committing a culpa. However, in doubles play, a ball striking a receiving player or his racquet and then landing bene in the court, may be returned from the bounce or from the fly by the player's partner not struck by the ball.

## EIGHT

The ball may be struck with any part of the racquet in any stroke provided it does not come into contact with the hands of the player. Once struck the ball is in play. Also, provided it does not strike the arm above the wrist the ball is also fully in play should it rebound back across the net from the receiver's court having struck that part of a player's hand grasping his racquet. However, it is a culpa should such player's hand be in motion.

## NINE

While the ball is in play no part of any player's body or racquet may touch the net, the player touching the net with his body or racquet causes a culpa irrespective of whether he is executing the shot or not. Provided a player is not executing or receiving service a player's body or racquet may extend over the net on condition he is standing in his own court.

## TEN

A shot is bene until such time as it lands in a player's court and is not struck before the ball touches the court floor for the second time. All parts of the surrounds of the court including Glass and Bulkheads, are areas in play from which a player may return a shot. The ball may be retrieved by the receiver from the Glass and Bulkhead before it bounces a second time on the court floor or surrounds. However a player may not go beyond the net into the court surrounds of his opponent's court.

## ELEVEN

The Brass is out of play at all times for both the players' feet and the ball and it is a culpa should either player or ball touch on this surface during a point played. At other times The Brass should be respected as a memorial symbol and treated as such.

## TWELVE

Doubles play shall include the Reeperbahn and rules apply for singles play, and service shall alternate between the serving players. The non serving and non receiving partner in Doubles shall not stand in the Memorial Zone.

## THIRTEEN

Upon a player winning his first point, his score is thirteen, upon winning his second point his score is fourteen, upon winning his third point his score is fifteen, upon winning his fourth point he has won a chukka. When both players have won three points the score is 'Laura' in the case of gentlemen players and 'Charles' in the case of lady players. In the case of the player winning the next point the point is designated 'my Laura' or 'my Charles' in the case of lady players, or in designating the point to an opponent it is 'your Laura' or 'your Charles'. In the case of mixed doubles the term 'Chalura' is used. A won game is referred to as a 'Chukka'.

The player having won the point 'my Laura' in winning the next point wins the chukka, should he lose the point, the score returns to Laura or Charles. A player winning five chukkas, wins a Clare except that he must win by a supernumerary of two chukkas and the chukkas continuing until such supernumerary is achieved. The first player to win three out of five Clares wins a Commodore which is the match.

## FOURTEEN

Play once commenced shall be continuous unless prevented by a contingency of rain or other more serious debacle which may require postponement in which case the umpire will designate a time for resumption of play.

Twenty seconds are allowed between chukkas. At the end of each Clare, the players shall change court sides, during which a rest of three minutes is allowed.

Interruption when this involves a discontented player's rage or other game distracting outburst, shall, should it extend beyond twenty seconds automatically terminate the match in favour of the contended player and forty seconds shall be allowed a player to replace his racquet or a garment in sudden need of replacement or repair and ninety seconds is allowed for doing a French professor. (refer to glossary)

One minute shall be allowed a player to regain his composure following a fall or other minor mishap.

Injury discontinuing play, the match is awarded to the uninjured player unless such player sportingly allows, with the agreement of the referee, for a fifteen minute recovery, or a resumption of the match at a later time, not to exceed twenty four hours.

Line disputes shall be decided by the umpire, who may overrule a line judge. In matches without an umpire, a culpa ball will be designated to the hitter by the receiver's non racquet hand being raised with the index finger pointing in the trajectory of the culpa. In cases where the culpa is close, the receiver may, following his pointing, raise his non racquet hand to indicate the approximate width between his thumb and the phalanx of his other joined fingers. A ball flying off into the spectators may be not be again used on court.

## Fifteen

It is incumbent upon every De Alfonce Tennis player to obey and be able to recite the Fourteen Commandments of De Alfonce Tennis:

Thou shalt not cheat nor accuse.

Thou shalt not swear nor put a curse upon another.

Thou shalt not kick a ball.

Thou shalt not throw a racquet.

Thou shalt not belittle nor insult an opponent.

Thou shalt not attack a spectator.

Thou shalt not upon court jump up and down in rage.

Thou shalt not upon court burp, eructate or expectorate.

Thou shalt not be rude nor scowling to the umpire

Thou shalt not falsely accuse an opponent of a culpa.

Thou shalt not impugn the name of a player or of the game.

Thou shalt not laugh at an opponent's error.

Thou shalt not covet another player's equipment or partner.

Thou shalt not ignore the manual of De Alfonce Tennis.

A player must at all times obey The Fourteen Conduct Commandments of De Alfonce Tennis and they may be invoked at any time at the discretion of the umpire, thus causing a culpa for the offending player or postponement, discontinuation or the award of the match to the non offending player. Where both players offend simultaneously or beat each other with racquets or fists, they cancel each other's culpa but the match may be declared mismatch by the umpire and the next seeded players supersede.

### ADDENDUM RULE

Although one hesitates to step forward and take a bow in this fashion, someone must assume the role which I hereby assume as the Honourable Founder who has in prolonged monastic isolation set to paper the elements embodying the superlative game of De Alfonce Tennis. In play with the Honourable Founder the following precepts apply.

A selection from Tchaikovsky's 'Capriccio Italien' played as the anthem of the sport. All in spectator attendance must be in evening dress, including officials. Prior to the match and during the initial reception festivities connected therewith, the founder will be addressed firstly as the Honourable Founder and thereafter as the H.F. Nor shall these letters out of pique, give rise to any insulting variation a prankster player may be vulgarly inventing.

Fourteen seats of the first row of the audience to the H.F.'s right are to be reserved for those top ranking in order of their ranking, the highest ranked player seated nearest the H.F. The on court dress code of the De Alfonce player is strictly observed. The highest known member of the legal profession with his appropriate robes surmounting his evening wear, shall be appointed as judge of the match, and before play commences, thirteen grunts conducted by such judge shall be coaxed from the gathering in memory of the original stalwarts of the game. The Honourable Founder shall be the first to serve.

Present should be a vicar, priest and heart specialist. All games with the Founder to take place following sunset. Strict silence shall be observed during actual play. The Honourable Founder shall not be allowed to lose, except in the extraordinary circumstances of an exhibition match held in the promotional interests of the game or where an outstanding world ranked female player is the challenger (game or where) and it would be considered unchivalrous for the Honourable Founder not to graciously be seen to be trounced.

## RANKINGS

In the top twenty, a ranking may be officially challenged and a challenge laid down by any player ranking not more than four rungs lower on the ladder. A challenge is formally made and registered in writing to the W.D.T.A. who is responsible for the keeping of the world rankings. In any such challenge the challenged player must play such a match on a date within three weeks. Failure for the challenged to play is forfeiture of his ranking to the position one below the challenger. By a match win, the challenger replaces the challenged in ranking.

In the next fifty rankings a challenge may be made by a player not more than nine rungs lower on the ladder. In the next one hundred rankings a challenge may be made by a player not more than fourteen rungs lower on the ladder. In the next three hundred and thirty rankings a challenge may be made by a player not more than twenty four rungs lower on the ladder.

It is at all times the challenger's option as to the choice of De Alfonce play, which may or may not include the Glass or Bulkheads, or Enceinte De Alfonce which must include the Glass and Bulkheads.

The names and addresses of the top one thousand world

ranked players shall be kept on file at all times, along with all paid up members of the W.D.T.A. who hold no ranking.

Even though your hale and hearty opponent flashes back at you his best injured look of scepticism, sickness or injury during play is not a forfeiture and play is stopped to be resumed another day provided play takes place within a further seven days.

## Foreign Languages

The terms used in play and scoring in this manual shall not be translated or amended for use in another language, nor shall grunts, squeals, other sounds or signs substitute for the word originals. Where a dispute may occur concerning the interpretive translation of this manual, the English language will remain the standard from which any interpretation may derive. No adaptation made in any foreign language shall empurple, impinge upon or impugn the English spoken origins of the sport and such in a match will invalidate the ranking of such player or players.

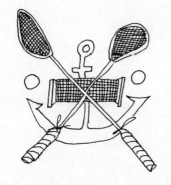

# CONDUCT

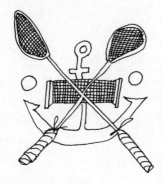

## The General Ambience

De Alfonce Tennis is a way of life and your striding upon court should reflect this in your every step and posture. The givenness of the De Alfonce player is to be fleet and light of foot, fluent of arm, graceful of stroke, accurate of shot, and masterly in executing disguise, but at all times remaining free of the arrogance that such accomplishment may provoke in others less possessed of the good nature of a true and fair playing sportsman. The De Alfonce player should exhibit too, an easily ignited gaiety and an unruffled but not smug demeanour. Perhaps not altogether unlike the pseudo aristocratic behaviour of Lord Charles, who at least in venting spleen, did so in a forthright and elegant manner.

As expertise can be so dramatically acquired in the game of De Alfonce Tennis, it can cause without warning utter havoc in the rankings with a resulting emotional hysteria possessing a player so deposed and such can cast an unstable character into an ingnominy which can affect his entire life. Therefore a resilient nature and an unquenchable optimism in adversity is a must.

Your behaviour on court should be as the word itself describes, courtly. Greet another player gaily, bowing perceptibly. When play commences do not hesitate to praise your opponent's well played winning shot which has left you wrong footed and frozen legged. There should be none of this seething bitterness to which so many players become prey as they lose one chukka after another to sorrily succumb in a Clare. Nor should you pretend that your muffed top spin cross court return was due to a slipped brassière or jock strap, loose shoelace or a searing pain in your ankle.

Particularly in mixed doubles play, a player will not chastise, scowl or growl, even in the mildest manner, at his partner commiting a culpa. Or take it as the opportunity to demonstrate how the shot should have been made. Such unsolicited instant lessons in how to wield the paddle or position him or herself not unreasonably disgruntles your

partner and is likely to further sour his or her play. Instead
a De Alfonce player will good naturedly, swallowing his
seething bitterness, offer a small word of bonhomie encour-
agement with a reassuring smile or pat or tap of the racquet
on the back, and will instead direct some jocular scorn at
the opposition.


## SERVING

Take up your position placing as the case may be, your
left or right toe at the Stern line. The feet should first rest
flat and astride and exactly up to but not beyond the merest
degree of discomfort. While so standing and feeling your
oats (refer to regimen, dealt with under such manual heading), you may nonchalantly strike the ball from your racquet, back spinning it to the floor and rebounding it into
your hand. This casually demonstrates your expertise as
well as being a preparation alerting your reflexes for your
impending serve. However, bungling this little drill does
rather produce smirks, if not on your opponent's visage,
then on that of the assembled spectators.

Service should commence with the ball in your lofting
hand and racquet firmly grasped at the nether end of the
handle. Then flex the left or right knee as the case may be,
leaning into the flexed knee with your body weight and then
return your weight back over the flexing of the opposite
knee. By lifting the heel of the left foot till the pressure of
your leg rests lightly on the first three toes, you may now,
once or twice, rock back and forth in a clock ticking motion
while wristy flicking the blade of the racquet downwards in
a to and fro manner, the blade describing the figure X with
a swooshing sound. Performed with a balletic flair such
motions awake the delicate rhythm which best alerts the
body to the split second execution required in the De Alfonce serve.

Prior to throwing the ball up, your eyes should glance

down at the swinging racquet, and also at your opponent receiving. You may also choose to be more deliberate, bringing the ball slowly to touch mid racquet then drawing your weight on the right flat foot, the heel of the left foot rising and toe pressure pointing to floor as the ball is thrown upwards. Your racquet should at the same time rise over your right shoulder and drop behind your back as if the racquet blade were to pat you between the shoulder blades. From this position the racquet then begins to accumulate its momentum describing its movement in an up and over arc till coming into concussion contact at a point slightly downwards past the apogee of your swing, the ball having been thrown up angled slightly forwards. The racquet at this time in the hand of an accomplished server may be travelling at a speed too fast to be seen by the naked eye. The body from its previous anchored position, now begins to pivot and as the racquet rotates, impacting on the lofted ball, the horizontal body weight tilts forward as the right foot moves towards the left while both feet rise to tip toes, impact being made upon the ball as the right foot comes adjacent to the left. Upon racquet and ball concussion occurring, the body continues to pivot, the right shoulder coming forward with the player now facing in the direction of the ball trajectory. Both feet now separate to take up an anticipatory position. The left foot being placed further left as the right places further right, the legs being ready to either advance to the net or remain set for a back or forehand return.

## The Nurt Ball

Unique to the game of De Alfonce Tennis, the Nurt ball is struck with the slightly elliptical top edge of the racquet which comes into contact with the underside of the ball at a point less than its full radius, thus administering to the ball a pronounced back spin which creates an air turbulence in which the ball hangs in slow motion to fall shallow in the opponent's service court where the ball's reverse spin on gentle landing causes it to roll without bounce.

To serve the Nurt, the ball is thrown up high enough so that the top edge of the aimed racquet can make impact on the ball's underside radius. Practice and a perfected concentration alone allows for skill to be achieved in this service. However, once mastered the Nurt service invariably results in a Zeke, descending forward into the service court it usually catches a receiver lax in his tracks behind his Stern line. Only an ultra alert and blisteringly fast player has a chance to spring forward to administer his racquet in the fying pan manner, to successfully finesse such ball back into the server's court.

## The Floater Ball

This ball similarly hit as the Nurt in service, is less pronounced in its back spin, the racquet impacting the ball at a point more than half the ball's radius. Such ball falling deeper in an opponent's court and producing some bounce. The Floater ball back spin shot may also be executed by a fore or backhand slice. It is a shot recommended when attempting to gain time to strategize, the shot when being returned by the receiver, having to be carefully compensated for as the De Alfonce Tennis ball tends, upon discharging the momentum of its spin on the racquet, to play downwards into the receiver's court or net.

## Racquet Wielding

In general court play, the racquet may be administered to the ball firstly by a carried through arm motion or secondly, by a swifter and considerably more skilled combination of arm, wrist and fingers, in which the arm, flexing at the elbow, in turn rotates the wrist as a swivel and

combined with the leverage of the fingers, results in utiliz-
ing the racquet in the manner of a lash. The flay shot, as
this latter is termed, is essential in returning a ball whose
lofted position, usually from the bounce, has passed beyond
the player. This stroke, because of its swooshing sound,
when executed at its most eloquent, is referred to as making
music. Such racquet wielding not being dissimilar to that
used in polo in sending the ball in the oposite direction to
the motion of your horse, enabling the De Alfonce player
to not only save the ball, but to return it fast and true at a
blistering pace, which, in cross court trajectory results in
leaving opponents lax in their tracks.

The backhand flay is a lashing shot administered from a
backhand stance, the surface of the back of the hand horizontally facing upwards from the handle of the racquet,
with the small and first index fingers splayed outwards
either side of the joined two middle index fingers, and the
blade of the racquet held horizontal on the back swing and
during its forward return motion, rotated to the vertical
upon making contact with the ball.

The forehand flay makes its music from the racquet
stroke describing a circle in which the blade winds down
from above the player's head with the wrist acting as the
swivel to bring the racquet snapping forward to make contact with the ball, a motion not unlike a jockey striking with
a whip his mount's haunches in a race.


## BUNTING

All shots at the net where the racquet is held and meets
the ball without being wielded by a full arm motion are
referred to as bunting. The player's hold on the racquet
handle, specially designed for the purpose, being choked up
upon, in order to gain leverage to absorb receiving the ball's
impetus as well as to help administer a directional force to
the ball in a short sharp manner.

## FINESSING

Such muted delicate oscillatory flicking strokes are executed closely at the net with the racquet held in a frying pan manner to either gently bump the ball over, or, held in the bread cutting manner in caressingly applying a modicum of top or side spin, to enable the ball to softly crawl over, or even along, the net top or in a dipping passing shot in cross court play, to speed the ball towards the Reeperbahn out of an opponent's reach. In doubles such strokes are executed by the player at the net while his partner takes up the plimsoll position on the stern line to cover the back court.

Warning: Such finessing strokes in their sophisticatedly exquisite execution, are frequently so excruciating that a player's tendency to both hysterically laugh and scream in such tourbillon, may also run him or her, the risk of committing a culpa under rule Fourteen which makes reference to 'distracting outburst'.

## THE LOB

Executed in De Alfonce play without the Glass, this stroke is struck with extreme top spin to give it pace and to keep it tight arced in as low a trajectory as possible but at the same time remaining well out of reach of an opponent's possible jump twirl smash return. The forehand lob is administered in the manner of the flay shot, with your racquet encircling above the ball's approaching trajectory and, in gaining its impact momentum, the blade is then lashed upwards over the ball. The backhand lob requires the racquet to be cocked back and in its forward motion resembling the ancient movement made by a farmer's hand when broadcasting seeds, the blade of the racquet is rotated over the ball in order to both loft it and administer top spin. Alas this latter stroke must be regarded as the most difficult to execute in De Alfonce Tennis.

## Off The Glass

Where bulkhead and ceiling play is de jure in Enceinte De Alfonce such shots off the Glass replace the lob and are used in defence against an opponent at the net. The stroke must be forceful in order to require your opponent to retreat deep to retrieve the ball. Always remembering that underspin will take the ball deeper into court from the Glass, and top spin tend to deflect the ball more directly downwards.

## Le Ricochet

In Enceinte De Alfonce play Le Ricochet refers to all shots which deflect off both bulkhead and ceiling before landing in court. Such shot is capable of putting the ball cross court in a nearly lateral direction. In singles play your opponent can, if near the net either finesse the ball cross court in reply, or jump twirl smash such Le Ricochet on the fly, which however may in turn be taken on the rebound off your own side or stern bulkhead, the heat of such play requiring the very ultimate in anticipatory strategy. Doubles play, however, allows for greater defence against Le Ricochet which is then best used as a disguising or delaying shot.

## Parry Riposte

In the full court length exchange of ball taken on the bounce with each player at or beyond his Stern line, such engagement is Parry Riposte, during which returns are kept deep to the Stern line of an opponent's court to prevent him from gaining the net. Such Parry Riposte is frequently long in duration, especially as a player rushing the net is immediately open lobbed, or in bulkhead ceiling play, forced back with a stroke off the Glass.

## BLAZING

In cases where your opponent has achieved a commanding position at the net and where your lob or play off the Glass is weak on accuracy, the strategy to be adopted is Blazing the ball, which is to flay it at the body area of your opponent. The ball must be driven extremely fast and is best aimed low with top spin, forcing a return into the net, or high with back spin, forcing the return out. Blazing will also lessen the receiver's ability in defence to dink the shot or give him a chance to execute an angled directional bunt cross court.

## ELLIPTOID LOB

This stroke, with side top spin, arcs the ball in a manner which propels it either in a right or left curvature necessitating the receiving player to not only anticipate its deepness but its deviation towards the Reeperbahn, so forcing an additional dimension to his defensive movement. Carefully disguised by the perpetrator so as not to be read, the stroke is made with an underhand lateral flay.

## DE ALFONCE ENCEINTE

Except for the area designated as Fifth and Madison named after the avenues, such emboxed play involving as it does all surfaces, including those of the Stern and side Bulkheads and the Glass, is the ultimate and the last word in De Alfonce Tennis. The interior dimensions of the overall court structure are in length, fifty four feet and in width twenty three feet, and the Glass being thirteen feet high from the deck. The nine foot wide service court area from the Memorial Zone to the Stern line reduces in length by two feet, being fifteen feet instead of seventeen. The net is attached flush to the wall and stretched even across court.

In taking service the receiver in his return of serve, may play the ball from the ball's bounce back off the Stern Bulkhead, or from the Glass or side Bulkhead. Such stroke off the Stern, which may also include the Glass, provides backspin, and projects the ball in a floating arc, which can vertically dink it gently close in over the net, producing a heart stopping moment in which a return can only be made by a caressed cross court Finesse.

## Street Adaptation

Not every De Alfonce player can afford to build his own court, especially in the more unadorned countries of the world and those where socialism remains popular. However as De Alfonce equipment is uncomplicatedly elementary, it is not outside the affordable bounds of even the more deprived of citizens and therefore may be acquired to be used in the simple street adaptation of the sport.

Dimension rules are varied to allow for different street widths, the curb stone, where such exists, acting as the boundary within which the Reeperbahn may be chalked or eliminated as the case may be. It is then only necessary to chalk in the stern and other lines to denote service areas and the Memorial Zone.

For Street De Alfonce purists, a piece of polished up old copper can do for the commemorative Brass, or for really poor deprived kids, tin or cardboard. But even in the case of the ordinary De Alfonce kit, there is provided a reasonable facsimile of the memorial Brass, and it is only necessary to unroll the pre measured boundary and line tapes to instantly establish the court. Or in the case of the adjustable variety of tape, such latter, also supplied with the kit, is capable of being cut to length where necessary. The net posts are also adjustable to allow for curb height variations, and in the case of the ultra de luxe kit, these of course are made of ebony.

City streets are an ideal venue where houses and buildings provide a longitudinal wind break. However on breezy days, and in the case of official play streets, protection from air gusts may be improved with the erection of screens to the back court.

Street De Alfonce will, undoubtedly, with those who outstandingly apprentice themselves in this way, provide a ladder upon which they may graduate upwards to avail of the full fledged variations of the De Alfonce court, to there distinguish themselves and from such, have the opportunity to emerge applauded as future world and Olympic champions.

## Gymnasium Adaptation

The kit for such adaptation contains net, net posts and anchoring, together with pre measured marker tapes which are adhered to the floor, thus providing in a few minutes a full De Alfonce playing court.

## Vaulted Glass Play

This is the rarest of all De Alfonce play, involving as it does either a longitudinal or transverse vaulted ceiling which curvature covers the playing court and provides a venue found mostly in medieval castles and stately homes Ideally the apex of the vault should not exceed thirteen feet All other rules of De Alfonce play apply in this exciting adaptation in which another directional dimension is added in play off the Glass.

## Two Handed De Alfonce

This amusing adaptation is more than a mere diversion and requires a racquet to be held in both the right and the left hand. Service is by the ball being thrown up from the face of one racquet to be struck by the other. There is the optional rule that play may be alternate, that is a player, having hit with the right racquet, must then hit the next stroke with the left. At Two Handed Random play, either left or right racquet may be used for any stroke. This game is excellent for sharpening the senses in both halves of the brain. And it does of course favour the ambidextrous player. It also prevents the muscle development of one side of the body predominating over the other which may disconcertingly give a lopsided appearance to your demeanour.

## Bis Ball De Alfonce

Involving two balls and refereed simultaneous service, both balls are played till they are both in Culpa, and all De Alfonce rules apply. This form of play may be adapted as well, to two handed De Alfonce and is recommended to players honing a supreme edge to their game. Or as a warm up device for skilled players.

## Paddle Tennis Adaptation

Much frowned upon by De Alfonce purists, but the De Alfonce authority recognizes that such a court provides a practice venue. And anyway, people, the moment perceiving eyes and ears, not to mention noses are taken off them, will transgress established rules and principles to suit their own book. On this larger court which has a higher net, play is permitted off the side and back screens, and all other De Alfonce rules apply in play.

145

## NAVAL ADAPTATION

This is one of the most ideal adaptations of De Alfonce. Especially on the larger naval vessels such as aircraft carriers, battleships and cruisers, where space may allow for several courts and major tournaments may be conducted. However, even on the larger amphibious landing craft, play can be made available in the tank well deck. Alas some of these heavy armoured vehicles may have to be bunched up to one end, or one or two left ashore.

On frigates and smaller vessels, with helicopter landing pads, these areas may be canvased off to set up suitable dimensions of the court while the helicopter is flying or perched somewhere else aboard. While at sea, the Captain of such vessel is entitled to the prerogative enjoyed ashore by the Honourable Founder, unless of course, the First Lord of the Admiralty or the Secretary of the Navy is aboard, when the Honourable Founder's mantle will devolve upon the latter. The De Alfonce flag will at the appropriate time be flown from the mainmast.

## STRATEGY

As it would take an entire bible of philosophical discussion to treat of even a fraction of the strategy employed in De Alfonce play, the least said about this subject the better. But tactics do differ and vary, being as they are an expression of the personal nature of the player. Therefore it is best to maximize those tactics which appear to benefit your play most, remembering to vary these as your opponent is in turn, constantly perfecting against them.

For the beginner, it would be as well for him to pay as much attention to his own and his opponent's clothing, carriage, conversation and demeanour, remembering too, of course that your opponent is paying you equal and similar scrutiny. Position rather than stroke error is usually the way a point is lost in De Alfonce as few shots, if you can get to them, are incapable of being returned. But between evenly matched skilled combatants, it can largely and excruciatingly be a contest of superior personality. Which alas may mean that if you lack a curmudgeonly reflective psyche you may get trounced in De Alfonce.

# REGIMEN

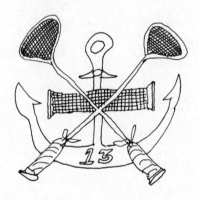

## FITNESS

De Alfonce Tennis, due to its long rallies and subtle strategies, requires an immensely exhausting concentration, which can, in skilled play, make it a devastatingly vigorous and tiring game involving as it does, extremes of physical, moral and mental energy. Therefore superb fitness is an absolute must to endure such threefold interrelated modalities.

It is always pitiful and assuredly disconcerting to see a player puce in the face, veins bulging at his temples, his countenance stricken with befuddlement, being trounced wrong footed off bulkheads and glass by a fit glacially calm player on top of his form and mercilessly executing his victim, who now disabled with exhaustion, is being ferried off court on a stretcher, and mumbling about seeing his lawyer for a malpractice suit against his doctor certifying him fit. It therefore behooves you to meticulously follow the prescribed training and exercises.

However, under no circumstances commence any of the following without first visiting your doctor and analyst for a complete mental and physical check up and written clearance for you to so commence, making sure he knows the exact extent of each exercise and metapsychological stress you are to undergo. Insist upon your doctor or analyst reading this present manual which might do him or her some good anyway and indeed may provide you with a partner with whom to play. In any event, unless he is the most crass kind of person, he will enjoy getting this present on top of payment of his big bill, especially if it is a leather bound and embossed first edition. But do beware, doctors have an uncomfortable habit of putting their stethoscopes directly over your wallet and he may of course insist upon adding a large reading fee to his medical charges. And while on this subject why not, with your priest, parson or rabbi, also have a moral check up. Which of course when the size of the donation is suggested, you may think you were better off just confining yourself to your expensive doctor and remaining contentedly immoral.


## AT NIGHT

The De Alfonce player should gently park himself on a firm mattress in a well ventilated room, before the midnight hour, and unless for part of the night, sleep alone, to be certain of achieving complete rest. And a word on sexual intimacy here. While this must be regarded as extremely good exercise, requiring as it does the use of every single muscle in the body, including, as other exercises do not, such tissues as the lips, tongue and private parts, nevertheless, when a major match is approaching it should not involve exaggerated gymnastic tricks, or dangerously engineered couplings over rickety furniture. Otherwise do indulge this activity freely but remain celibate (the rule does not apply to ladies or masturbation) for two days prior to any match involving a championship. And in the converse, also make sure that you have had a carnal coupling within the seventy two hours prior to such match. This tends not only to infuse confidence which can linger with you through the further forty eight hours, but also leaves you suffused with the inspiration of your fantasies to be indulged, with even a little light whipping to bring you down a peg, following your triumphant garnering of laurels.


## MORNING

The De Alfonce player rises and shines at any time between six thirty and eight a.m. and by nine the latest, on weekends. However seven fifteen is a good average time to aim for. For the first five minutes after waking be careful and slow in your movements till the body has had a chance to loosen and disintegrate any gouty uric acid crystals formed overnight in the bursae of the joints. And too, the muscles of the heart must acclimatize to pump in the vertical again.

If you are possessed of a terrace, and the weather is suitably clement, step out and take a look at the sky. This alerts the pineal gland which in turn alerts your hormones. If the air is reasonably clean, inhale a deep breath or two and give yourself a couple of firm thumps on the chest, which will help make you aware that miracle of miracles, you are still quite pleasantly alive despite all the dirty rats trying to do you down in your life. But don't thump too hard. Your thymus is in there.

## The Breakfast Time

This crucial most important meal of the day is one which should be consumed in sacred calm. And your beverage and victuals, as recommended in the diet given in this manual, should be presented exactly as you would like them. Don't hesitate to shout remonstrations to your butler should something be amiss. And if you have anything like the half arsed version resembling Austin, mentioned previously in these pages, don't for god's sake let him raddle you with his own personal career concerns or spill hot coffee over your wrist while pretending to serve you breakfast in bed. Make sure there is no grease on the bottom of your tray from his own big fatty breakfast or that your saucer and plate is aflood in spilt milk. All matters, which although not immediately life threatening, do nevertheless provoke a needlessly disagreeable irritation when your body is preparing itself for that day's De Alfonce play.

Although some butlers are hopeless they are frequently less a pain in the arse than a resentful wife. This same sentiment of course applies to women De Alfonce players and their preferment of a lady or houseboy in ready waiting, to a pompous monotonous husband making morning noises resembling the Russian revolution in a nearby bathroom.

To sum up, this ideally should be a time to write your diary, examine your fine art auction catalogues or just daydream while avoiding the bad news in the daily newspaper. The hours immediately following the first opening of the petals of your sleep, is when the spirit awakes anew, and is when your perceptions are at their most sensitive. And by allowing them to give free rein to their focusing, you prime both body and mind to be in full readiness to play this day, the match of your life.

## THE BOWEL

Perhaps more than sleep, calm or anything else this organ wreaks a profound influence on your existence. Only because your life, alas, wreaks a profound influence upon it. Ideally the bowel should be moved at morning time following breakfast, and bells, horns, hoots, caterwaulings and sirens should not you dismay.

In such difficultly obtained utter tranquillity, have available a large glass of cold limestone percolated water to sip. Have reading material to hand, such as Medieval and Pre Raphaelite art catalogues, these being most restful to the spirit and eye and enormously helpful in causing these vital moments to be leisurely and easeful. Make sure the movement is complete, but do not sweat or strain over such egress. And positively never never jump up in the middle of something still emerging. To be seen with one hand hopelessly wiping behind and the other twisting off the door knob in your rush to answer the phone. It is thus that, prior to entering your bathroom, you do not fail to have stacked sufficient pillows over this instrument or be carrying with you the radio controlled variety. Of course it behooves you to ignore your carefully wrought tranquillity in tropical countries where a mamba, cobra, scorpion or tiger snake might be gliding or crawling at you over the floor. In such lethally dangerous case, drop what you are doing and while you are leaping somewhere fast in a chandelier direction for safety, don't forget in the case of the mamba and king cobra, to draw your feet up high.

## The Bath

Following moving the bowel, the bath is an essential requisite for both relaxing and soothing the body. Keep the water temperature at a perceptibly warm but not hot temperature.

To sensitize your skin to the pleasure of being warmly enfolded, provide bubbles from a goats' milk preparation approved by the De Alfonce Tennis Association and submerge yourself, head and all for a few seconds, remembering to close the mouth and hold or blow out breath through your nose. Such hippopotamus antics loosen catarrah in your eustachian tubes allowing you to free such passages by a little vigorous hocking and spitting.

Having wallowed about sufficiently, take a kneeling position in the water and soap up your privates well, and with such forefront lather, deep massage and vigorously wash the adrectal area. All in all you should arise from the waters with a glow stimulating you to take on the first of the day's activities.

## The Shower

Such deluge should be reserved for your second ablution of the day in removing the sweat of your play. Here the water pelting on your head invigorates the neurons and perhaps allows you to mull over where you went wrong in the match. If no such problem assails you you might then beneficially luxuriate ensemble with your mixed doubles partner when the washing of your inaccessible parts may be achieved.

## TOWEL DRYING

Vigorous massage towel drying is the first of your day's inadvertent exercises, and a large good quality absorbent bath towel emblazoned with the De Alfonce approved emblem, is essential. With a vigorous pumping motion, start two handed with the face, mouth and back of your head. Next place either foot in turn up on the edge of the tub, then holding the corners of one end of the towel, throw the remainder forward over the whole leg. In a massaging manner push and pull the towel with your arms, starting with the underpart of thigh and extending to the knees. Then stretching forward, do your shins, ankles and toes and calves. The chest and stomach is next, and the privates last. In the case of gentlemen, the balls are, in a gently wagging manner, flopped to and fro.

Standing fully erect again (any tumescence in another area being all to the good) grasp a suitable stretch of towel in both hands, throwing it back over the head. Your hands holding it there firmly, draw the towel back and forth in a sawing motion across behind the shoulders. When tiredness is felt, the towel is then dropped and grabbed again under-arm and the exercise continued with a sawing motion down the entire spine to the bottom of the buttocks. Use every last ounce of strength to complete this. Of course if you've already been doing towel exercising all your life and it's never done anything for you, it's only because you've been half arsed about it.

## GROWLINGS AND GRUNTINGS

This activity must not be confused with throat clearing, hocking and spitting, but is in the nature of pure voice production. Albeit your facial contortions will be unbecoming and certainly anyone overhearing you will think you have thoroughly gone bananas, as well as being possibly dangerous. This must not you deter, for loudness is a necessary quality of the exercise. Awaking in you as it does primitive instincts which rid of negative repressions and shakes the rust off your psychic chains.

Do not under any circumstances turn your growling into discernible words, especially those which may be obscene, paranoid or threatening, although in the nature of this exercise, you are bound to occasionally do so. It is therefore a wise precaution to have your copy of the present manual open to this present page, in case an unsympathetic and calculating mate thinks he or she may now at last have sufficient evidence of your instability to call the gentlemen in the white coats to sneak with their strait jacket into your abode, and there through keyhole or other tiny aperture, witness your insane sounding clamour, to then suddenly crash in upon your privacy to take you in the manner of a Lord Charles away to incarceration while lawyers declare you incompetent. Warning: this exercise for ladies, although toning and firming the muscles of the face, and unless it is practice for divorce proceedings, is an ungraceful one to indulge.

First exercise: Shake the head vigorously from side to side while at the same time bubbling air through your lips and resonating loudly in your nasal passages. This should not continue for a period of greater than seven seconds, as there is a danger you may not be able to stop.

Second exercise: Growl and snap the jaws at the same time as rotating the neck left and right, lifting and stretching the chin while so doing. Continue for thirty seconds.

Third exercise: Grunt, letting the sound emanate from low in the voice box. You may beneficially shake your shoulders at this time. But refrain from letting the head make an affirmative motion as this appears you are asking for a banana.

Warning: Do not conduct these exercises in front of a mirror as there exists a report of a Bangokok player actually breaking his mirror in an attack upon himself.

## TOE FOOT FLEXING

Standing, place the heel of the right naked foot four inches laterally apart from the left naked foot. With toes pointing in a thirty degree direction, and a light pressure keeping them in contact with the floor, rise up on the toes vertically and then return foot flat to floor. Repeat 15 times with each foot and increase by two every two days till reaching 120. If attempting to achieve superlative championship fitness or for ladies needing an aesthetic improvement to the lower leg, the exercise should be repeated at a ten minute interval.

## TOE RISING

Place both naked feet about a foot apart, the toes facing outwards. With the momentum gained with dipping the knees slightly forward and down, rise simultaneously on your toes as high as possible, returning flat foot to floor. Commence gently with twelve, increase by two every day till reaching seventy five. When you have achieved 50 daily, alternate with toes turned inwards. Strengthening gained from this exercise is especially beneficial in springing to receive serve or in sidestepping a lady's kick or in a fast removal of self from a teller's window when robbing a bank.

## ANKLES

Your entire game can depend upon this miasma of cartilage and ligaments. Being a hinge joint in an extremely sensitive area and more than any other joint in the body prone to fickle disorder and sprain it should always be kept at the supple peak of condition. As with the well working of all joints much depends upon the synovial fluid maintaining a lubricated gliding action of one internal surface upon another.

Fortunately the ankle is part of the anatomy easily exercised at one's quiet ease, and while the foot is in either a shoe or slipper. While at your evening fireside or even parked by the television when this latter is less than riveting on your attention, get in the habit of alternately rotating your ankles with your toes pointed ceilingwards and describing a circle approximately six inches in diameter. Start with seven rotations to the left and the same number to the right, and increase by two every second day till you reach 25 for each foot. For superlative championship play the exercise is repeated at an interval of one hour. At the same time the shin muscle may be directly exercised by hooking the toe up and down, twenty being the number of times and repeated again at an hourly interval.

However a small caution here. Be mindful that this exercise is liable to be excruciatingly irritating to anyone else in the room, even your butler and most especially your spouse for whom it can quickly become a basis for an accusation of mental cruelty.

## ACHILLES TENDON

This vital band of fibrous tissue, although the thickest and strongest in the body must on no account ever be allowed to weaken through disuse. Once you hear the utterly unforgettable sound of this little item attached between your Os Calcis and Triceps Surae snapping in two, and get stabbed with the anguishing pain, you will think a broken leg is a tickle in your bifurcation in comparison. And get ready for much immobility, for this infirmity can land you up to your arse immovable in plaster for weeks when only the grunting and growling exercises of this manual are likely to do you any good. And remember, the Achilles snapping asunder, can be done to you even while gently waltzing at the annual De Alfonce Ball.

Therefore if this tendon is in the least rusty, mild massage should precede your first exercise, and this, always done before your day really starts. For there is nothing like becoming hopping mad over the yet again breakdown of your private or apartment elevator to send you fuming out your front door to hysterically step straight in early morning canine merde on the footpath and then in an angry frenzy to tear this utterly indispensable cord of fibrous tissue into ribbons. So in your less troubled times always remember to particularly concentrate your mind on this tendon's existence when doing all foot and leg exercises.

## CALVES

These muscles receive their workout while you are doing your general standing leg movements and daily walking. Strengthening and conditioning may be increased by rope skipping or by to and fro and lateral dodging or reversing of foot to foot while on your toes. In short, simply jumping and jigging all over the place. Hopping backwards on the toes also helps, but never, and as with your foot dodging, do these some cool morning on your small balcony on the twentieth floor. For you could find yourself crashing arse first through your pathetic shrubberies and free floating head downwards towards the flattening of innocent executives on their way into their black limousines, and all due to the unexpected fibre rupture of the Plantaris muscle and tendon. This diminutive item layered between the Gastrocnemius and Soleus calf muscle is highly susceptible to injury and in the more mature gent, wants to be treated tenderly especially by those taking up De Alfonce Tennis late in life. Small as it is, when this sliver of tissue snaps, even at its narrowest point, it's like being explosively slammed on the back of the calf with a baseball or cricket bat.

If you have never even sensed the existence of this long but tiny bit of anatomical equipment nor a twinge of its being stressed, not to worry, for being so small a muscle, it is entirely possible you may have been born without one.

## KNEES

When you talk of your joints, this one presents a nice complicated puzzle of three articulations in one, involving both a gliding and rotation movement, and giving you of course, all those awful creaks you hear in a deep knee bend. However, powerful ligaments make it one of the body's strongest joints.

Nevertheless, the Cruciform ligaments which keep the tibia and fibula attached to the femur are crucial, and if broken, your leg will go out from under you like a dandelion snapped in two. Therefore it behooves you to lavish tender care in keeping this leg swivel in first class mechanical order.

Always be slow and gradual in warming up this joint before subjecting it to full playing stress. This may be done by simply alternately extending each leg horizontally in front of you and raising your foot up and down through ninety degrees. Never let the knee get ice cold. Avoid any violent lateral knee twist or spin. Don't displace cartilage or bust your Bursa by coming down with the edge of your racquet on your patella. Astonishingly, being knock kneed, can be to your advantage in De Alfonce Tennis, not only giving you additional on court agility but a certain directional disguise in movement.

## THIGHS

As the position of the leg in De Alfonce play is nearly always with the knee bent forward either in making or in anticipation of receiving a shot, much depends upon the condition of the front muscles of the thighs. But if you are completing in full all the other leg exercises as instructed, these big muscles which include the Sartorius muscle, the longest in the body, as well as the Quadreceps extensor which form the contour front of the thigh, will nearly take care of themselves.

However, this area, although it must be kept hardened and strong, should not be let get over bulged, tending in such state not only to be extra baggage in your swift travels on court but also to be distinctly unflattering to ladies especially if the leg is bowed or bandy. If you have a past history of Cossack dancing, soccer playing or as a ballet star, and your thigh amplitudes are splitting your De Alfonce toggery, gentle jogging and stretching will help tend slenderize you in these upper underpinnings.

Note of warning. These muscles are prone to cramp, especially at moments following an intensive long day of De Alfonce play, when you are in a state of relaxation and nonchalantly gathered among friends at your favourite street side cafe, having your De Alfonce non alcoholic aperitif, and then, as one of these big muscles knots suddenly like a thunderclap, you disappear off your chair, your two hands hopelessly grabbing at the offending area and at the same time from under the table, trying to explain in your agony that you are only temporarily hors de combat. The worse nuisance being of course, gathering pedestrians and that inevitable busybody on the outskirts of the crowd who invariably calls an ambulance. This is why, in order to save such embarrassment, you should first make sure before disappearing under the table to shout loud and clear.

'It's nothing at all folks.'

A massage or sauna or both, following a strenuous match helps avoid such cramp. But if you are in this manner so convulsed, instantly feel for and find the knotted muscle and knead it with both hands from the centre to unlock the contracted fibres, at the same time slowly stretch the muscle back to its normal extended position. Always then remember to stand up, and bow to assure your companions that nobody yet is about to step over your dead body.

## THE HIP

You may not have this knowledge at your fingertips, but the ilio femoral ligament keeps you, with its enormous strength, standing up straight. However, many have found out that this enarthrodial or ball and socket joint can really fast put you in need of a cane and make you look like you are on your last legs. Therefore it really behooves you to long term keep this astonishingly manoeuvrable hinge, top notch.

Because of the protective security it enjoys in its location, there are few specific ways of concentrating on hip exercise movements. Stretching the trunk is one of the better ways of warming up this vital axis without your arthritic agony grinding you suddenly stopped. And for the still athletically mobile, jogging and walking constitute the basic efforts to maintain a good level of condition.

Warning: A dislocation here will really put the ligamentous cat among the cartilaginous pigeons. With squab everywhere for dinner. So. As with the knees stay well away from games such as Rugby and American football. Not only do these games risk throwing this vital area out of joint, but the contusions they engender can make this internal leg rotator look to the surgeon operating, that it's been through an automobile crushing machine.


## THE BUTTOCKS

In and about this area which forms the prominence of the nates, although such muscle fibre is regarded as histologically coarse, there is nevertheless a good bit of informal satisfying fun to be found, both for commenting upon and under suitable circumstances, for penetrating reflection not to mention whips and lashes. So you'll want, as a De Alfonce player, to really keep these eye catching conspicuously curvilinear muscles looking their best.

A nice casual, and at the same time sensually pleasant

exercise, is to tense and untense these muscles. Thus adding to their hardness and conformation, while you wait, as it were. Ladies however are warned that this can invite unwelcome attention as nothing is quite as inciting for the De Alfonce player as these globes, flexing in their glory under some silken close fitting fabric.

Deep knee bends, back arching in the standing position, or with legs flexed up apart in the supine position when the buttocks are raised off the floor, develop these essential muscles, as well as help strengthen the lumbar area of the spine. Although your opponent's present fitness cannot be easily determined from the amplitude and definition of the buttock curvature, nevertheless a gluteal flatness in the area can definitely mean your opposition isn't worth a kick in the arse.

## The Abdomen

As the superficial and deep muscles of the abdomen not only assist breathing action but also compress the abdominal viscera and are the highly useful means by which you urinate, defecate and vomit, and indeed for De Alfonce ladies, pop out babies, the basic daily exercises for this part of the body are not to be missed by the De Alfonce player. The only excuse for not doing these is, if you are, while mountain climbing, bivouacking on a ledge narrower than your body width, from which the sheer fall is greater than thirty metres.

As the belly is highly vulnerable to being a fat collecting area, it is much to your advantage to be mindful that instead of its spilling over in disagreeably flopping tumbling tiers of fat, that wearing a flat muscled abdomen, with your intestines tucked firmly in their place, not only makes you look good in your general context but also will give you a sense of benign well being. In maintaining top playing form, a minimum of one hundred and twenty sit ups per day are in order. Should you stretch left and right to touch your toes while your legs are splayed apart at forty five degrees, the number of sit ups may be reduced by a quarter. The number of sit ups should be commenced at three and improved at the rate of two additional sit ups every other day. To avoid stress on the hamstrings the back of the knees should be kept at least six inches off the floor. And never, repeat never, should you allow your number of sit ups to fall below the minimum requisite of thirty five per day.

## THE SPINE AND BACK

Sirloin steaks come from this area in cattle and will give you an idea as to what is required in the way of exercise to keep these muscles healthy, and your discs from slipping and ossification at bay. Out of a usual total of thirty three vertebrae, you really want to be most daily mindful of the twenty four movable ones. Nor forgetting that tunnelled through them is your message sending spinal cord. Which, if ever sheared by a violently displaced vertebrae, will certainly stop your toes from tingling.

General exercises consist of those standing and supine. In the former, spread the feet apart and rhythmically bend, keeping the legs straight, to two handedly touch each toe. When straightening up, place hands a moment on hips and rock twice to squeeze the kidney area. In the supine exercise, bring the feet together while flat on your back and lift them backwards over the abdomen, chest and face, to touch behind your head, your toes tapping the floor a distinct three times. Additional strengthening comes from holding your legs a second or two suspended in front of you as your legs are lowered back to the floor. Beware that wind, without warning, may break from you at this time, as indeed it may tend to do in any of the vigorous stomach exercises. Such blasts if they do not distinctly enthuse others, certainly are all to the good of yours truly as indeed such creative emissions seem to unaccountably buoy up the spirit.

A third exercise, in the supine position, is to raise each leg alternately up and over till the toe of the stretched leg touches a spot outwards from shoulder. This should be done a total of forty times. Warning. None of these exercises must be attempted if you feel a disc is drifting from its mooring or other spinal untowardness is on the brink of revealing itself.

As exercises for the abdomen, spine and back, tend to be awfully dull, and are, as in the case of the abdomen, priority exercises that should never be missed, the number of repetitions of these exercises may be varied to suit your mood of the day but always kept at a number necessary to retain a plateau of fitness from which top fitness may be achieved without causing stiffness or busting your coccyx.


## SHOULDERS

Although eschewed in general in De Alfonce training, various light weights are used to exercise arms and shoulders. They consist of small hand held spheres weighing eight ounces, one pound and two pounds respectively, such acting to compensate for the extra strength required in strenuous court play. Plus keeping you fit for hugging and squeezing your nearest and dearest not to mention breaking the ribs or backs of those you detest.

Six pound dumbbells are for the fully fit player and lesser weights for those achieving fitness. While the weight is held in each hand, rotate the shoulder in the manner of the butterfly swimming stroke, the arms describing an elliptical circle as they are stretched to the greatest circumference. The rotation then proceeds in the same manner in the reverse direction. This exercise prepares the shoulders and arms for De Alfonce Tennis' most vigorous strokes, the serve and the jump spin twirl smash.

The exercise should commence at six and increase by two every other day till the number sixty is reached. Such training is also helpful to a lady looking to maintain a certain curvilinear resilience in her hemispherical eminences. In this respect she may choose to use a slightly heavier weight in her right hand, to offset the curious phenomenon that the left eminence is usually more prominent than the right, although such disparity she may wish to retain as an intriguery for those who may be so by, abstracted.

## WRIST AND ELBOW

Aside from making you adept at face slapping, these joints, with your wrist being the most vital, administer your racquet at its most strategic in top class De Alfonce play, much in the manner of the virtuoso violinist. As the wrist execution of many shots relies more on speed and finesse than it does on strength, no better way exists to flex, extend, abduct, circumduct and adduct this joint while it hangs from the elbow, than actually swishing your racquet through its playing motions. For rhythm and grace, you may while doing this, provide yourself with suitable orchestral accompaniment on your gramophone, using your racquet as a baton to conduct.

If you are careful not to knock people's hats off, the casual twirling of your De Alfonce walking stick while promenading the boulevard will also practise you. But such antic, seems to incite in other pedestrians a resentment in thinking you're flaunting a smug self importance, and some, so incensed, may actually attempt to grab your stick from you. Should this inappropriate street contretemps happen too often, you may instead prefer to, indoors, employ a six to ten pound dumbbell attached by cord to a stick which weight is then wound up and down by the wrists and hands. Provided you don't let your half arsed butler try to put together such a contraption, not only will this exercise help avoid De Alfonce elbow but it will soon move your watch strap out a notch or two and you can be well assured that when your sleeves are rolled up, no boulevardiering busy-body will be eager to accost you with their highly disagree-able interference.

## HANDS AND FINGERS

Being so obviously in use throughout the day, and indeed at night too, such occasion requiring, it is easy to forget that fingers need to be frequently stretched and articulated. And especially for the hand to be stretched open and fingers spread to their widest, exercising them in lateral movement.

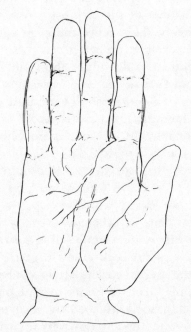

*The Hand Of
Horatio Josiah De Alfonce Adams IV*

With the fingers then so extended, draw them together in a claw like motion without fully tightening them into a fist. A morning and evening dosage of thirty five, followed by one hundred rapid full fist tightenings from an outstretched position of the fingers, should keep you ready to put your hand to most anything. All the above are suitable as fireside exercises, and may be completed by massaging in a De Alfonce approved hand cream. Again be warned that another in the room will find this activity peculiarly annoying, and especially in the not quite top notch restaurant folk so irritated in this manner, have been known not only to pull the carnation out of your button hole but to also splash your vichyssoise in your face.

## NECK

In the brain and in under the skin of the throat are pineal and thyroid glands, and it will do no harm to keep them caressed in a resilient environment. Even with all the curiosity attracting phenomena of this world turning you around to look, this is an area often neglected in exercise. Through this neck area goes all vital electrical communications and energy supply, therefore it must be kept internally fat free and externally jowlless. Any viscid coagulate bunging up of the carotid artery to the brain region can not only sail you headlong into premature senility but can also keep you from being a clear thinking person which is much demanded of you in conceiving the intricate anticipatory strategies necessary on the De Alfonce court.

Providing you are leading a reasonably active life, forty rotations of the neck in a circle as far forward and sideways and backwards as you can manage, and then turning the head to point your nose at each shoulder twenty times, should, morning and evening, be sufficient to keep this area supple and strong. Exercises should start with only the gentlest motion of the neck and increasing gradually to full extension. Don't be alarmed by the creaks but nevertheless really watch out what the hell you're doing here. Some of these muscles are extremely temperamental and can easily decide to discombobulate themselves without preamble. Also be aware that if done as fireside exercises others in the room may think you are annoyed with them.

## BRAIN

As the De Alfonce player takes his eccentric identity from this organ, it will be appreciated that its psychic condition is equally as important as its physical. And even though it isn't, for the sake of your alert demeanour, a whole lot should appear to be going on in here. Since this principal ganglionic mass of the central nervous system is used to determine the steps you take to keep other parts of the body in championship order, it's best to keep other De Alfonce players thinking this is exactly what your brain is doing.

To be given ultra consideration, is the thalamus, hypothalamus and pituitary, even though hardly a thing can be done to improve them beyond the condition they were born in. Although a hard slam on the head from another player's racquet may deprive you of your appreciation of music for a while, you will still have left plenty of brain matter with which to coordinate metabolic and physiologic activities in the rest of the body and to keep your hormones humming and your satisfactions in life, monitored.

However as the brain cells do not divide or change other than to deteriorate, actual physical improvement to the organ is improbable during your lifetime. Nevertheless this ganglionic mass is capable of improved will power, and by multiplying suitable images, intensifying luridness of thought. Basically it is rather less a case of providing beneficial things for this organ than it is of preventing awful things happening to it. But it still follows, that this whole area warrants some external stimulation for its own good keeping, even if it requires you occasionally to stand on your head in order to get freshly oxygenated blood up there. Rumours in recent scientific circles hint that somewhere in the area of the dorsal brain is an aging clock ticking away your lifetime, and although you may be in no hurry, you will at least want this measuring instrument to be accurate and not unduly jump the gun with a big release of aging hormones which wave adieu to your animal spirits.

With the grey and white matter encased in the cranium, as with the rest of the body, it goes without saying, one eschews anything which leads to its softening deterioration. Cold water splashes on the skull and brushing hair and teeth vigorously every morning is at least a routine helpful in this, and like the polished windows and the well kept lawns surrounding your house, will give you a look of being bright eyed and bushy tailed. Which is at least better than appearing forlornly bent, busted and, in the parlance of Lord Charles, buggered and knackered.

## EYEBALLS

Like the fingers, these pigmented organs, if still projecting images of the outside world through your vitreous humour, on to your retina, will be taken for granted as already being in good De Alfonce playing condition. Operated by a multiplicity of muscles, and transmitting your reflexes with the speed of light, it behooves you to believe that nothing could be further from the truth.

Crossing and uncrossing your eyes to focus on the tip of your nose is an excellent all round exercise of these essential globes. This again is a random exercise easily practised while sauntering along the boulevard. You will of course attract stares and sudden looks from other pedestrians which should not deter you. And as your sudden cross eyed appearance gives you the demeanour of being somewhat deranged, it actually, in crowded cities like New York, Lon-

don, Rome and Paris, pronto clears the pavement ahead and
will invariably discourage muggers, pick pockets, and beg-
gars. However do make sure that immovable, non pedestrian objects are not immediately in your way, as it takes a
least a second to fully refocus the eyes to their norma
perception.

Eyelid fluttering to exclude and admit light also benefit
the eye by exercising the contractile curtain of the iris, bu
be careful where you do this, as it can be misinterpeted
especially on the boulevard where if you are at all comel
in appearance you are likely to attract highly unattractiv
and disagreeable folk looking for an uninvited feel of you
flesh.

Occasional crying, especially of the sobbing kind help
keep these orbits debris free. So that persons don't thin
you've just gone bankrupt or are otherwise all washed up
this is best done in a dark cinema with a suitable tear jerkin
film. But if such is incapable of moving you, you will hav
to wait till something heartrendingly sad enough happens
meanwhile striding out in a cold wind, when available, may
if nothing else in this world grieves you enough, succeed t
make the eyes water.

### LARYNX

Much affecting the general disposition of the spirit, a
well as your joie de vivre in De Alfonce play, this orga
will certainly fall into pathetic disuse if, off court, you be
come a curmudgeonly old souse, tucking yourself away b
your fireside, silk encased in your De Alfonce pyjama
aplomb upon your satin soft, escutcheon adorned uphol
stery, and licking your accumulated wounds over a co
glass of champagne and plucking from the Meissen plat
placed by your butler, a caviar canapé while your ears so
up the blissfully lyric calming strains of Tchaikovsky
'Capriccio Italien'.

Instead roust out of your doubtful peace and get on the telephone and invite someone somewhere. Of course everybody has already made plans but don't be cast down by the third consecutive refusal and then pour yourself another glass of bubble sparkling, palate delighting champagne and call for your butler to spoon out some more caviar from the big can nestled nearby in the crushed ice. Of course at the fourth person turning you down, it is an immediate exercise of the larynx to shout down the wires as loud as you can, that they and all the previous folk you have called, can go and do to themselves what they have been long desirous of doing to their bitterest worst enemies. And give yourself a few seconds to regain your composure and take comfort from the fact that on the remainder of your champagne you won't give two hoots or a howl about anybody. But will have meanwhile, adequately exercised your larynx.

## The Lungs

Elasticity and lack of catarrhal congestion plus a pink cleanliness exhibited in your final autopsy is what we look for here. As no De Alfonce player has ever got hot enough to smoke, we hope this physically scourging invention, need not now be further railed against. However, even if you don't emit this white gas out of your head, dust of all sorts, as well as noxious fumes, in particular those industrial, should be avoided. And in this avoidance, nasal breathing is helpful, but your city town house or apartment should be also equipped with a clean air filter to give your lungs a night time rest. And never sniff a strange bottle to see what's in it.

Nothing is as beneficial to the lungs as long distance running and the copious deep inhalation of volumes of fresh pure country air, or the presence of pine forests or an orchard upon which your bedroom windows should open. In judging yourself to be in a constant source of good air examine the nearby tree branches for the presence of lichen.

173

## The Heart

Alas this anciently evolved, forty or so cubic inches o
hollow muscular organ is the one thing you've got to keep
going at all costs and wherein you don't want to burst a
conduit or have a hernia. And sorry to say that all these
marvellous exercises so far provided in this manual
although they help nicely, they are simply not enough to
keep this big pump fit. Even though this oxygen irrigato
is working all the time, it needs more exercise than any
other part of the body. Indeed the equivalent of a six mile
run at least three times a week. But for god's sake if you'v
just leaped an apoplectic mile off your office chair or up ou
of your satiny sofa in disappointment over all your previou
hopping and skipping you have faithfully performed from
this manual, don't treat this distance as being anythin,
more than an ideal to be aspired to and for which you ma
indulge plenty of weeks to achieve.

But once starting out to do so and adding on the miles
nothing could be worse for your De Alfonce image tha
being driven to taking up marathon running, whic
although unquestionably puts the heart into hyper fitness
nevertheless produces in you such a highly objectionabl
smugness at your physically superior fitness that it can onl
but make you slightly repulsive on court. Remember tha
De Alfonce Tennis, once you have perfected your gam
will do all that is needed in seventy minutes of play t
maintain reasonable heart muscle fitness. And provided thi
organ is kept beating, you will be happy to hear it is nc
the be and end all of the cardiovascular system, as ther
exists a chemitelecommunicative sensitivity in the body
tissues which automatically adjusts to meet the needs c
such living matter and astonishingly can, when necessary
even stimulate the new growth of blood vessels. But nc
yet, alas, a new heart.

## THE KIDNEY

Although Lord Charles frequently availed of his kidneys
to demonstrate his chagrin at various disagreeable aspects
he encountered in his shipboard travel, basically this double
barrelled organ is part of your drainage system, removing
from the body as it does, accumulated impurities of a nitrogenous nature dissolved in water. Were you ever to see this
extremely delicately designed organ working in microscopic
close up, you would think twice about the purity of the
fluids you drink.

To keep the kidney fit, not only must you daily exert the
body a minimum of three miles in the locomotive fashion
of walking but also quaff at least five pints of spring pure
water to keep this organ from regressing in any way. Long
periods of immobility are anathema. And the frequent need
to take a piss helps.

## THE LIVER

Alas the liver is profoundly fundamental to all your well
being. This unbelievably complicated network of cells not
only forms a vitamin supply depot, and the body's guard
room against infection but also is vital in breaking down
the mild poison in the alcohol of your favourite De Alfonce
approved champagne. Big and silent, this brown entity
plays a major role in excretion, purification, storage, meta-
bolism and when it goes awry, will give you, with your
blood seemingly pounding around your brain, one awfully
dreary headache.

Having been so warned this organ is temporarily on the
blink, you'll soon know it is not a time to be out there
pounding away on your six mile training stint or perspiring
as you finesse a cross court passing shot in your De Alfonce
arena. And you are hereby strongly advised to pronto
supine lie low taking honey for energy, until this part can
mend itself and render your eye whites white once more. At

the same time remembering all organs respond well to a friendly soft squeezing and caressing motion, so it helps, even while bed ridden, to regularly roll gently side to side.

## The Casual Exercises

On the assumption that none of your organs is causing you discomfort these fortuitous flexions can be enacted anytime and in any suitable place they are thought of, including on trains and planes when these are prolonged in transit. But on short trips they are not appropriate, as they could make you appear to be suffering from some travelling phobia. Nor are they suitable to be done in places of sincere religious worship or during weddings and christenings. Particularly avoid doing them at funerals where someone might take it that your grief had destabilized you. And be especially aware to keep still in the crematorium where bumping the wrong button can be a grossly embarrassing hazard. Always remember you are one of the select as a De Alfonce player, and who, as an inheritor of the 'Fourteenth's' quite wry demeanour, never invites the obtuse attention of another.

In journeys longer than an hour and a half and especially while in flight above altitudes of 30,000 feet, don't be afraid of getting up out of your seat when the turbulence warning light is definitely off, and in your own limited aisle space do your stretching, knee to shoulder and other flexing and bending exercises. But in front of a whole jumbo load of passengers, do not, during the more suspenseful moments, block sight of the in flight movie. Avoid also the entrance to galleys or lavatories as someone emerging especially from the latter, might get the idea, that having kept you waiting for so long, and on the verge of being unable to contain your contents, you are so enraged, that you are about to bust them one.

Always take the view that you are setting a good example

to other passengers. Except in first class areas, there is unlikely to be more than one or two other De Alfonce players,
who, god forbid might suddenly all get up at once flailing
limbs at each other. And do remember hijackers give themselves away by suspicious behaviour, so don't demur when
told to sit down by the staff air crew. Such disobedience
especially on your higher flying aircraft, where cabin pressure may be at its maximum, could lead to major disaster
if it were thought necessary a bullet be used to subdue you.
Better at such times to peacefully settle in your seat and
gainfully pursue the quiet massaging of your De Alfonce
elbow.

## The Workout

Having the previous day got your doctor to pronounce
you ultra fit, don't be alarmed that this, when not involving
De Alfonce play, should ideally cover four hours, as some
of this period engages you in peaceful indolence. The time
chosen to begin your workout should best follow at least an
hour's constitutional on the boulevard, and therefore should
not be delayed beyond mid or late afternoon.

If you have, as a member of a health club, university or
corporation, or ideally, privately, the required facilities and
equipment, present yourself in such area, in athletic gear
comfortably suitable to the weather and temperature. On a
resilient mat, spend at least ten to fifteen minutes stretching
to limber up all parts of the body. While thus maximizing
your physically flexible capabilities, you can also at this
time spiritually meditate.

Now you are ready to perform selected calisthenic
routines from the De Alfonce manual. Complete as many
of these as you can in twenty to twenty five minutes. You
should now be gently perspiring and ready to undertake
your mile run in under, but not faster than six and a half
minutes. As your fitness builds, thinking of what you will

do to an enemy at this time reinforces your endurance, and will enable you to add a longer distance, increased by two hundred yards every other day until you achieve four miles.

Following all runs, a five minute walking rest should follow, during which, if you are member of a club with other talkative members, hold your hand up to discourage them from engaging you in discussions during such ambulatory intermission. In the event of the more pushy type, when you see them coming in your direction, pretend you don't and move off. There is nothing worse for your routine than when some intellectually good intentioned person, steers you off in philosophical pursuit of some eternally imponderable question no amount of talking will ever solve or change. And in the case of someone proposing some ridiculous deal, which, unless it really sounds damn good, don't hesitate to throw up both hands and shout, no, no no.

It is now time to make your way towards where you conduct a further twenty to thirty minute session of fencing or boxing. These two endeavours are perfect for honing your performance on the De Alfonce court, being sports where reflexes are required at their highest and are instantly rewarded or punished. Do however as a gentleman protect your jewels and as a lady be careful to insulate your eminences. You will now have just about reached an equal point of exercise as you might expect from an hour's vigorous play of championship calibre De Alfonce. Increasing the previous regimen of exercise by one third should improve your stamina to cover an additional hour. All play beyond this point will be exhausting no matter how fit you are.

Taking heat is the next part of the workout procedure, winding you down gently. But do not enter the hot room until resting for a further sufficiency. Then spend up to fifteen minutes supine in a dry heat of 140 degrees, followed by seven minutes supine in steam. A five minute power shower is your next item. This consists of being blasted by a powerful jet of water over your muscles from about eight feet away. Gentlemen should beware of their eyes and gonads, or if a lady, eyes and eminences. Being rammed by such jet, can either bruise or worse, for gents, knock items off you. In not taking the spout, you may substitute a cold shower. Then dive into the pool and swim fifty yards in a relaxed breast stroke followed by a further hundred yards in the crawl and finishing with fifty yards in a slow back stroke. Depending upon the standards kept by your club, wash off either the algae or the chlorinated pool water under the shower and slowly dry off in the De Alfonce manual manner.

When dry present yourself to your masseuse or masseur. Then wrapped in warm sheets with one below and one on top of you, and together with towels, either lie where you are or present yourself so wrapped upon a deck chair or settee. Again this is a severe danger time for verbal interruption from another member not only wanting to let you know he's really alive and still absolutely mesmerized by his reasons for living but even that he's prospering in such behaviour. So cover your head with a towel to prevent interruption of this most vital period of rest and peaceful contemplation. You will be astonished that you will absolutely go out like a light and sleep for at least fifteen, twenty or thirty minutes. And prepare for being somewhat disorientated when you wake up, acquaint yourself again with your immediate surroundings, and be careful rising, doing so deliberately and slowly. Heart attacks have been known to strike at such times. And although usually fatal, the pain is brief.

## Post Workout

You will now have combed your hair, donned your street clothes and refreshed by your regimen, will be viewing the world from your vantage point of revitalized confidence. It is time to now proceed to your club's bar, lounge or tap room to take on liquids. And so please make sure such place provides the approved De Alfonce drink, which consists of pure grape juice taken mixed in equal amounts with mineral water in a tall glass packed with ice cubes, and upon which have been squeezed two quarters of lime juice. A window from which to peer out upon the passing population, complements a savoury cheese, pretzels or nuts taken with your drink. Above all do not have an urgent engagement which might shorten your enjoyment of this profoundly replenishing moment of leisure.

Of course now is also the time you might tolerate your previous interrupter, who should be made pay for your drink, although this small penalty may make it hard for him to take up the previous metaphysics he was pondering to proffer and to kick about with you, in the abstract.

## TAKING TIME OUT

If you have made yourself a nervous wreck with hypochondriacal worries about the possible failure of one of your organs or have paid overly studious attention to any of the dictates or exercises of your De Alfonce manual, and so worked yourself up into a frazzle, it is then absolutely essential to calm your synapses with an utterly foppish devil may care, indolent day, starting with a two hour, butler served breakfast session in bed. This is forgiveness time in which the stern diet admonitions of this Manual may be overlooked, and the blueberry pancakes, pure maple syrup, sausages and Irish bacon may be dumped upon you in plenty, and washed down with freshly ground and brewed coffee. With the day's newspapers surrounding you, and a soothing symphony on your gramophone, now is the time to remind yourself of all things you should implacably ignore in the world. Before you later start regretting what you have done on this day.

Having so dined and further luxuriated through your

ablutions and as the hour approaches one p.m., a quiet four mile walk is in order. Avoid unpleasant looking streets and concentrate on any fine or even eccentric passing architecture. You may even spend part of your afternoon at the zoo watching gorillas, bears and seals and while doing so, eat ice cream. Then really spoil yourself by repairing to one of your better hotels, where the manager knows the whys, wherefores and musts, of the most soothing of all ceremonies, the taking of afternoon tea. Lapsang souchong with lemon of course, should be preferred. And cake too if you feel your liver, after what you have just put it through, can take it.

Your day should end with another short stroll to your club where you relax in a twenty minute steam bath followed by a gentle one mile swim alternately using the crawl, breast and paddling backstroke every fifty yards. Dried and dressed repair to have your De Alfonce drink, again viewing pedestrians, done from your favourite vantage point just a few feet above their passing heads.

Now is a time of decisions, as to whether to have a simple salad, and follow this with apple or blueberry pie. Or to set off to gobble down fatty heart degenerative portions of bone marrow on toast and herring in sour cream. However, whatever you do make sure you have read one of the better evening papers in the club library and see if you can find a partner, with a similar amount of leisure as you've got, for an hour's billiards or snooker.

Stroll home if this is convenient, and if you're not to be assaulted by muggers. But growling in the previous fashion suggested in the Manual should sufficently deter any of these marauders. Before retiring, leave your butler instructions for morning, and listen to a symphony, Fauré's 'Requiem' being a suitable soothing music to put the cares of the day to rest. You will be astonished that upon laying your head upon the pillow, although you have not done during this day one single thing to improve yourself, or the world, you will nonetheless, your conscience untroubled, drift instantly off to sleep. However, don't be surprised if towards morn, you have a nightmare where your enemies are chasing you in a twenty six mile marathon run. And as your shoe laces are loosening, you are quickly getting out of breath.

### At the Office

Having indulged to the hilt taking time out, it's now appropriate to consider the place where you may be spending the major portion of your life. You will already have had an early morning warm up getting there, side stepping through sidewalk pedestrian traffic and rotating your neck muscles to ogle certain attractive people.

Following the first hour at your desk and having opened up and answered urgent mail, and provided they haven't got you squeezed in a closet to do this, you will now be ready to avail of your seven by four foot exercise mat on your office floor. If the bare athletic expanse of this looks too gung ho, it may, so as not to be intrusive, be covered by any good Afghan rug. Indeed such can add a certain touch of the exotic. Upon such mat can be carried out all the supine exercises in the manual including standing on your head, supine leg waggling, and random leg extension and contraction with its thigh criss crossing in all directions. During which latter, gentlemen should be aware of these sudden scissor movements crushing testicles. But even crushing an occasional odd ball is justified, as it is anathema for the body to sit at a desk for more than forty minutes at a stretch.

In mat exercises you are again reminded that these exert upon the stomach certain pressures which make ill fragrance by wind breaking a distinct risk. Therefore a well ventilated venue is a must if your office comrades are not to exhibit a distaste in your company. Not to mention a dozen or so other reasons why they might hate your guts, or think they smell a dirty deal.

## Stair Climbing

Steps are often safer and frequently more fragrant than elevators, and you may tell a De Alfonce player by the fact that he climbs all stairs two steps at a time. If three steps at a time are being climbed you may be certain you are watching the super fit De Alfonce player in action.

While descending stairs, limit yourself to four steps at a time. And make sure in such latter activity the steps are strong enough to withstand your heavy impact and that the stairwell is not impeded by someone carrying a sofa upwards. Remember too that long uncleaned carpets can send up asphyxiating fumes of dust with every downward step.

These stair exercises among other things, give strength to execute jump smash shots and also concussion training for landing back on court after such strokes. It also conveys a not unpleasant feeling of take off and flying. But make sure the latter is not prolonged and that as a result you are ready to join the permanent ranks of the infirm De Alfonce player. Albeit that in such company you may still remain able to trounce all comers.

## Weights

Weights used should not exceed six pounds, except that in a fit player, he may double this in a specific strength exercise affecting the arms and shoulder to improve administering the explosive strokes of serve and the jump spin twirl smash. Nor to be overlooked, is the free style swinging of weights which are lifted, flexed and extended at will in all and any direction from the shoulders while the body is at the same time bending every which way. The danger here is disorientation and dizziness or a weight flying loose or worse clonking you on jaw, temple or dome, and knocking yourself out. So in all such training, do be ultra careful, not to, light as they are, drop one of these gravity prone objects upon your unprotected head or toe.

## CHAMPIONSHIP CALIBRE

Alas this is another kettle of De Alfonce altogether. At this level of match play you will be called upon for the utmost in endurance and strength. Weight training should be increased slightly and in your running training, now include seven sixty yard sprints. Footwork should now involve whole body movement exercises based on the lateral and longitudinal lunges in play. They build up your super endurance and help perfect form. Warning. Your office is no place for these as it will make you look like a victim of decision making stress.

## DIET

If you have had infelicitously nitwit parents or guardians who fed you plenty of salt, sugar, fat and soda pop, not of themselves poisonous, but can, in their accumulated combination, along with other up to date noxious colouring, flavouring and preservative substances, do your organs no good, and which you might have studiously avoided, then you can only now hope you haven't stumbled upon the De Alfonce Manual too late.

To find out if this is the case, again, for the umpteenth time, insist your doctor read this and give you a thorough twice over, before you indulge this Manual's advice. You may already have passed the point of no return and now require medically advised if not administered sustenance. And can but place your hopes in cryogenics giving you a chance to rehabilitate when science is finally bringing the deep frozen dead back to life.

The world now has so many actual poisons, seen and unseen flying around these days, and freely available in the most appetizing things to contaminate you, that even cannibalism is a likely lethal diet. These toxins risk knocking, not only your organs out of action, and putting you irretrievably in the compost heap, but also can loosen your nucleic acid molecules on some of your chromosomes. This in itself is not the most heinous thing that can happen but if such tangentially tempted molecules are sent flying and are replaced by others of a disturbingly unsuitable nature, they can in due course, make your heirs wish they weren't born.

Alas to avoid all such damaging particles, you would need a day and night sleuthing staff of atomic physicists and biochemists. So best instead, to get a decent gardener to start your own De Alfonce garden and apply the general principle of attempting to put genetically untampered with seeds growing in uncontaminated soil, and when sprouted, into your mouth, with the least lapse of time, application of condiments, or animal fatty cooking. And if, following the considerable expense in remaining a De Alfonce player, you can still afford, on top of your butler, the presence of a loving hand to present these, you are indeed blessed.

## THE BREAKFAST SETTING

Taken between the hours of five thirty and ten a.m. or at the rousing sound of the roosters on your country estate or at the more uninviting noise of street cleaners and garbage collectors in the city, this is the most important meal of the De Alfonce player's day. And it is when your large private income can be at its most acutely beneficial. Providing, as it can, the essential blissful circumstances free of nagging voices, irritating noises, folk in a hurry, or the sight of any spiritually disturbing intrusion upon the vistas out your windows.

Disagreeably hot or cold temperatures are anathema. Of

course you can overdo the aesthetic appurtenances to an extent which may make them seem cloying. However, this is usually unlikely, for even when you find yourself creaking comfortably in your wicker chair, breakfasting semi al fresco within the glazed protection of your terrace, and purring beneath the leaves of your grape vine, often your guinea fowl and peacocks will choose this exact moment to bellow unnecessarily. Or decidedly more inconvenient, an aerially gymnastic swallow flies in under your glass canopy and anoints your croissants and coffee with a panicked deposit or two.

However, if your butler has served you with a pair of De Alfonce sound proof attested earmuffs and a bird dropping proof umbrella, there are still other deadly serious circumstances to be avoided. Especially if you have taken your broker's advice to buy a previously promising stock which you now see in all its sickening horror, emblazoned in an unpleasant newspaper headline, as having plummeted irretrievably into its worthless depths. In such black void you'll be glad to contemplate the resale investment value of your exquisite antique silverware, and your onion pattern Meissen sitting on your damask table cloth. And a damn good breakfast, arriving at that very moment, just might distract from this major disagreeable. Unless, of course, you now encounter the pre eminent hazard of the morning mail. Which if you are confronted by any legal or illegally threatening words, is always made much worse by being directly addressed to you. Such vexations just as you are loading a dollop of dripping honey on your toast, although not fatal, can be a malediction to the digestion, and utterly binding upon the bowels. Which latter are also at risk at being disturbed by the ringing of your unlisted bedside telephone which invariably happens when you are aseat in your ablution throne room, while you are totally content with your otherwise unoccupied mind. Usually you have no one to blame but yourself for stupidly disclosing your number in some momentary overture of friendship to someone who wouldn't be in touch if you weren't a celebrated De Alfonce player.

It should already be adequately apparent that planning ahead is a must in your breakfast undertaking. And if you can get your butler, fully dressed, or cook, at least in her best kimono, out of bed early enough, and if either values their job, it is possible, by a few rehearsals, to extract from him or her a decent replica of the ideal De Alfonce breakfast. But count on there first being a long rough road to travel. With the coffee brewed with unsuitable water, or your toasted bran muffins burned black, or not toasted at all, and crumbling to pieces. And the wrong sized spoon served with your cereal.

## THE BREAKFAST INGESTION

Don't whatever you do, pin up this photostated page of this Manual in the pantry, along with your present explicit instructions in order to catch your butler's or cook's very likely extremely sleepy eyes, for these words are likely to wake them up just enough to subtly make your breakfast miserable. And remember, wives or husbands, unless they actually genuinely like you, will make even your worst bungling butler or cook seem like a saintly treasure. And you might very well be better off to struggle creaky limbed out of bed and do all these things yourself, squeezing oranges being particularly good for wrist strengthening.

Beginning course: Firstly your fruit juice must be extracted with as much of the pith as possible remaining, or such residue put mixed in your glass. From the pips or seeds, choose three of the fatter ones. These to be served separately, and eaten first, as they may distinctly not be as tasty as you would like. In fact many varieties taste awful. And may not even be that good for you. But here we are concerned with conditioning yourself to eat as much vegetable, cereal and fruit fibrous matter as possible, without your butler thinking you have a cog loose or bolt missing, but alas it is a prejudice you will frequently suffer as an eccentric De Alfonce champion.

In the event of a temperamental member of your staff breaking the squeezer, which might be better for you anyway, your peeled fruit segments can be arranged in an attractive star, with such as a black cherry or strawberry in the centre. For your sugar free compote, your larder should provide for a menu of figs, pears, guava, apricots, wild strawberries, blueberries, lychees, pineapple, melon, or stewed prunes. Unless you want to test the quality of your dentist's fillings, do not attempt to chew the latter seeds unless your teeth are your own and the enamel on them is diamond hard.

Second course: In a bowl at least five inches diameter and three and a half inches deep, deposit one level half inch of pure bran, one half inch of mixed raw oats, laced with raisins, finely chopped dried fruit and nuts, one quarter inch of pinhead oatmeal, then add three eighths of an inch of freshly milled wheatgerm and upon these layers should be sliced a whole decent penis length banana. With a small measuring pitcher add to the mixture, a half inch deep pure spring water, topped off with sufficient skimmed milk to keep the remainder moist.

Because of the need to preserve cereals for the long periods they await your jaws in storage, or stand on shelves before your unsuspecting butler's hand reaches to purchase them, be sure they are conspicuously De Alfonce approved for aromatic freshness and are free from any ingredient which may taint its purity. Although food companies claim this prophylaxis is for freshness and for your ultimate good, in practice they receive the fresh financial benefit first and leave you with the unbeneficial stale residue. Indeed the mould and mildew they try to prevent, might be better for you. But in case it's not, don't try it.

Third course: This may not, by the most recently discovered nutritional standards be the absolutely best thing
for you, but potted meat, spiced with just a hint of garlic is
a nice change from your usual breakfast. Although it will
be a real test for your cook or butler, nevertheless herein-
after is included a note on the making of this great York-
shire nutritious delicacy.

Firstly, it requires the beef to be hormone free and with
every speck of fat removed. Cut the beef up in small
chunks, cover air tight and long simmer. Removed from
cooking, it is then double ground fine, a task always disliked
by the kitchen staff, especially those whose hearts are not
in their work. The paste is then seasoned and put in pots
and sealed. It may then be deep frozen to await eating. And
on a piece of wholewheat toast, it is a tasty morning delight.

Other third course items may consist of broiled tomatoes,
or an occasional kipper. Or if you feel in any way well fed
already, you may instead slather your honey in the comb,
including the wax, on to your various whole wheat or bran
breads.

Beverages may consist of a glass of mineral or pure spring
water, grape juice or as you can get just too nutritionally
pure for your own spiritual good, coffee or tea. And with
these latter one does adopt the attitude that occasionally one
needs something enjoyably bad for you to provoke eating
that which is unenjoyably good for you.


## LUNCH

Except for an apple eaten whole, including core seeds and
skin, or a bunch of grapes or raw carrot, the De Alfonce
player takes no lunch. If bidden to a restaurant and facing
being less than gracious in not taking victuals for which
someone else is paying, and in order that the bill be not
kept so low as to infringe the amount of a good waiter's
deserving tip, you may order some caviar with a sprinkle

of lemon juice and perhaps a sprig or two of parsley on the side.

In the eventuality of having to be seen toy further through the meal, three or four delicate asparagus tips with the tiniest weeniest dollop of mayonnaise, or a trifling amount of foie gras garnished with parsley might meet the contingency. If the meal extends into a more lengthy affair, and everyone seems to be full of a gustatory bonhomie, you can knock off a fruit salad or in extreme circumstances of a deal near consummation, a very lightly made crêpe suzette. But two and a half hours must elapse before a training exercise or De Alfonce play.

Of course in people's homes it is difficult to ask your host or hostess as to what else have you got, like caviar, that I can sparingly eat. And so you may have to move food on your plate from one position to another in order to pretend you are shovelling it in. In an emergency to show your plate clean, whisper to your hopefully hungry fellow guest to see if he or she would like to switch plates. They won't, but at least this conversational opening, leading to a discussion of cardiac arrest, will keep you from noticing your hostess noticing you not eating her food.

### DINNER

Provided you have avoided an invitation to lunch and upon the presumption that the full training schedule or playing routine has been that day fulfilled, the De Alfonce eccentric champion may treat this as a time to moderately stoke up as it were.

Since the human alimentary tract is much longer and its stomach acid much weaker than that of the animal carnivore, it behooves the human mammalian to be a herbivore in eating habits. Nevertheless the occasional allowance should be made for food regarded by many nutritionists as being food unsuitable for man. Otherwise you could sit around for hours wondering how the hell you avoid what's on the menu. And you should not worry unduly if, once a month, you take on, in one fell swoop, a cheese burger with a fried egg on top. But with atherosclerotic plaque in mind when you cautiously eschew such burger, a sample selection for dinner follows.

First course: A sliver of smoked salmon or similar smoked fish enticed with a squeeze of lemon on wholewheat bread will, when taken with a glass of draught Guinness or De Alfonce approved champagne, do you no immediate irreversible harm. Nor indeed will an avocado or a bowl of vichyssoise, and you will thus be put in a ready mood for your next major savoury step.

Middle course: If you have refrained from the cheese burger, and abstained also from roast beef slab or thick steak, then you can munch your teeth into some lean fish, or shrimp and any combination of the following selection: Spinach, potato, brown or wild rice, artichoke, parsnip, turnip, cabbage, bamboo shoots, aubergine, beans, chick peas, lentils, lima beans. Don't be afraid to drip onto your mixed mushroom lettuce salad a small bit of pure safflower, corn or virgin olive oil, nor be bashful to include some garlic, chopped olives, green or red pepper and generous helping of onions. Beets which can make you pee pink can also be taken at this time. Radishes, if and when available, should always be part of your meal. Also find something upon which to put a little horseradish sauce this root containing as it does a few nice trace elements. Pure grape juice, glass of wine or popping a beer can be your tipple here.

Last course: This traditionally involved a pudding or sweet in which sugar usually plays a major role. Provided you understand that refined sugars are not good for you, which knowledge alas affords no protection in the eating, you can at least feel that were you starving, they would keep you alive awhile. However, you can upon your once a month chosen occasion, eschew your usual fruit salad and give yourself blueberry or apple pie à la mode, which are at least minusculely less tending to gum up your interior workings than are meringue gateau, and orange caramel custard. Anyway if it is only that one day in a month, you may tackle a rhubarb ginger sorbet, or pears in wine jelly. But you would be best off with an apple au naturel.

## BEST ETHNIC MEAL

For top condition championship De Alfonce play, Japanese cuisine with its raw fish, sushi and sashimi is to be preferred. Otherwise, the general rule is that the staple diet of primitive and savage peoples is invariably better than those you chew in honour of the more advanced modernized countries.

## ETHNIC MEALS NOT ENCOURAGED

If your dietary principles cannot sustain you to avoid them, and you succumb to a departure from the De Alfonce way of life, such sin and risk of putting your arterial system into eventual occlusion, can be lessened by avoiding the ethnic meals hereby listed vaguely in order of their detrimental qualities and in brazen disregard of the fact that some of them may taste damn good, and indeed, may even be occasionally beneficial: American Fast Foods, French, German, Polish, Hungarian, Czechoslovakian, Russian, Chinese, Indian, Italian, Mexican. This list however, if there is not a Japanese restaurant around, admittedly does rather leave you chewing your fingernails. And in such case, you should be especially aware, as you trace your famished rapidly weakening steps through the streets, not to desperately jump into a passing Jewish Delicatessen, and to there indulge a mustard slathered hot pastrami sandwich on rye, a kosher hot dog, and lots of lox and bagels which you yawn down with a beer, along with less harmful helpings of pickles, and cole slaw.

In order to avoid the problem of evading ethnically un-suitable foods, the De Alfonce lunch box or picnic bag can always be discreetly carried containing the ingredients listed in the per day essentials. Held on your lap, this may be discreetly resorted to, although in the better restaurants, it may require considerable practice to avoid being conspicuous.

## THE PER DAY ESSENTIALS

Four tablespoons full of bran, or even better oatbran and oatgerm, one whole orange, one apple, one small raw onion, one avocado, two radishes, three shrimp, one clove of garlic, half a pound of grapes, two pieces of wholemeal bread, and one large erect penis sized raw carrot and banana. Five pints of water. Your avocado should be sprinkled with a chopped mixture of herbs which may include marjoram, rosemary, mint, thyme, dill, mace, sage, sorrel, fennel, parsley. And don't forget some fresh basil.

## PARTIAL FASTING

Do this once every three weeks or seventeen times a year. On fasting days drink the required amount of water and consume at least four of the above mentioned essentials. If such fasting makes you feel good, it may be increased in frequency subject to your doctor's nose being again forced into these pages and his approving, or even joining in with you. But only fast if it fills you with satisfaction.

## FOODS FORBIDDEN

The De Alfonce player automatically forswears for life the pure use of the following: sugar, butter, eggs, cream, chocolate. Of course it does not count if someone slips you one of these unbeknownst, but be assured they do not have your welfare at heart, and although they may not be out to immediately murder, there is no slower or surer way of killing you.

### ALIEN SUBSTANCES

With the exception of inoculations against disease, the De Alfonce player in good health eschews all pills, tablets, potions and suffers all pain.

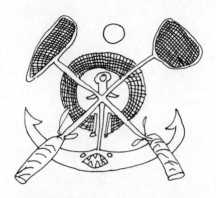

# MATTERS
# MISCELLANEOUS

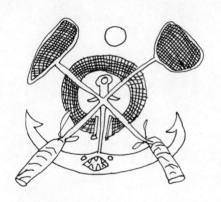

## While Travelling

De Alfonce Tennis players will always have accompanying them in their luggage their De Alfonce gear. By availing of the inadvertent exercise given in the Manual they can maintain their physical condition provided that they walk four miles per day or run two. In hotel rooms and the like they can practise play against the wall and windows and upon towels or other softening materials, do their sit ups and floor exercises. In certain De Alfonce approved hostelries it is arranged, that upon identifying yourself as a player, a room will be provided you with automatically disappearing furnishings to allow you such practice.

A note of caution: During a growling or grunting exercise, while in awfully foreign countries where you do not know the language and no one will understand enough of yours to read the Manual, take the precaution of always carrying prominently in your luggage or upon your person a foreign edition of such manual in the relevant language. And if you are burst in upon by paramedics or police, you will have the pertinent paragraph to point to in their own lingo. But do already have the book open at the pertinent time so that you may point or grimace in its direction, remembering that in foreign tongues everything you physically do becomes highly exaggerated, and the police are likely to play safe, immobilizing you completely and any motion of the eyes or lips or grimaces are likely to accentuate the reasons the police think they were right in apprehending you in the first place.

## Disease

With exception of the venereal, De Alfonce players on top of their form have little to worry about in this respect. However there will be the occasional time when some bug gets into your guts or otherwise invades and puts you supine. But during such time, make sure you at least mentally exercise by playing imaginary games of De Alfonce for forty minutes each day.

## HANGOVERS

Although rarely appreciated by the victim, the pain of a hangover can be curative of the spirit, bringing upon the body a temporary physical depression, which teaches you a lesson on many levels and especially not to drink too much again. Let twenty four hours elapse before serious De Alfonce Tennis play recommences.

## THE OBSCENE PHONE CALL

You may wonder what on earth or the deuce this has to do with the superlative game of De Alfonce Tennis, and you would be right to so wonder. However, as this form of sexual contact has proliferated so widely it must be assumed that one or two De Alfonce players may be so involved. As this may happen during the forty eight hour period of celibate abstinence prior to a crucial match, advices must be presented to cover such contingency.

The rule is that no De Alfonce player must instigate the contact during the said celibate period. However, if he or she is in receipt of such a call, he or she is absolved of the rule and may passively attend to the exercise of his or her privates for the purpose but he or she should not provoke or be the aggressor to his or her opposite number in such call. And under no circumstances should De Alfonce Tennis references be used in such conversations.

## SMOKING

As the hick up in the sticks, when asked by Burt the ex alcoholic if he smoked answered 'Ain't never got that hot' so too ought this to apply to you.

Under no circumstances should this chimney activity be taken up as a habit and if taken up it must be abandoned as soon as possible. Being mindful that it can take as many as ninety days for the residues of smoking to disappear from the body once smoking has stopped, will give you some idea of the powerful and addictive quality of the habit. And if you tend to be slightly spineless and weak in character, only the adopting of a carefully planned long term method can help you cease and desist. Unless of course the previous aspersion cast upon you, angers sufficiently for you to stop smoking forever as you read this.

One such self help method for breaking the habit is ceremonial and a log book is necessary. From the number of cigarettes you are smoking each day, subtract one every other day, this being placed in an ornate and elegant box upon which is emblazoned the De Alfonce emblem (refer to merchandising) and the box becoming a commemorative reminder of your ritual. The log book will be the history of your triumph. If you are smoking two, or however many, packs a day (twenty to a pack), place in your ceremonial box one more cigarette every other day and in the case of two packs a day it will take considerable days till you are smoking one cigarette. And if your smoking butler has not pilfered too many of these, each week you will have a bigger and bigger batch of cigarettes to ceremonially burn. The importance of this arrangement is to keep yourself smoking steadily and gradually less, allowing the body to keep pace and adjust gently to withdrawal. At the same time oxygenate the lungs with De Alfonce Tennis, starting with forty minutes each day slowly increasing the amount played to an hour and ten minutes. Succeeding at the above method of stopping may make you unbearably smug but it will also firm up your moral fibre which will be sure to have been softening in your past life.

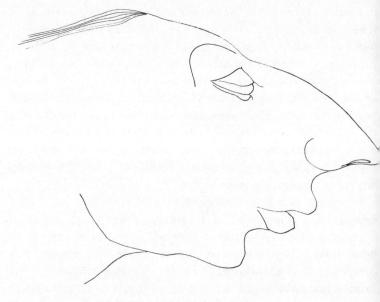

THE MALE DE ALFONCE PLAYER

## SNUFF

A pinch of this now and again does no harm. But for god's sake don't take it up as a habit. Enveloping yourself in these brown clouds and staining your cuffs, hankies and moustache.

## THE OLYMPICS

All De Alfonce players should keep their attentions alive to the establishment of De Alfonce Tennis as an official Olympic sport, having regard for the status they must maintain as players, so as not to contravene any qualification required by the Olympic Committee for eligibility to compete as a De Alfonce player upon De Alfonce Tennis' acceptance as a major Olympic sport, in which the many brilliant of you are destined to become champions.

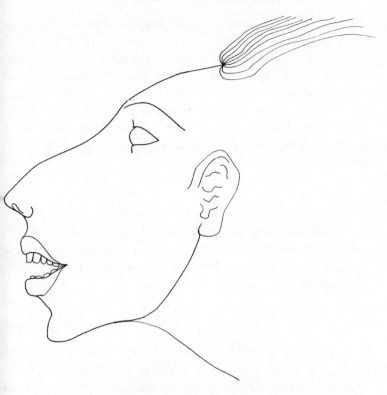

THE FEMALE DE ALFONCE PLAYER

### CHAMPAGNE

As this is the preferred wine of most De Alfonce players, arrangements are made with the blenders of the best specially selected grape to ferment this beverage. The De Alfonce Tennis wine committee convening at least once yearly to wine taste and approve both growers and fermenters, and to designate the licensing of and to declare any vintage years. Such wine chosen shall display upon the label the De Alfonce emblem with the following legend.

DE ALFONCE TENNIS
SPECIAL RESERVE

201

Twenty-four cases per annum of such wine so above approved shall be placed at the disposal of the Committee, twelve cases of which are reserved annually to the Honourable Founder. In the same champagne manner, special arrangements may also be made for De Alfonce Tennis approved beers, wines, spirits and liquors. Mineral waters, soda pop and new first time invented beverages, not necessarily alcoholic will be accorded most favoured nation treatment on a first come first served basis.

## MORAL PRECEPTS

De Alfonce Tennis Players are not to have a low moral opinion of women, nor are women to have a high moral opinion of men. Thus shall the two sexes come to respect one another.

## TATTOOS

If you adore your De Alfonce this much and want to run the risk of blood poisoning, hepatitis, lasha fever or other dreadful disease unpleasantry by having your skin punctured in this manner, so be it. Provided such tattooing is not of a risqué nature it is not required to seek permission for use of the De Alfonce emblem. But under no circumstances should the emblem be used upon an area of the anatomy which might tend, even by flexion, to discredit the sport.

## THE DE ALFONCE TENNIS PRAYER

Let all of us De Alfonce players, be of those whose blood flows fast in life and who shall use from our beloved game such shots and finesses that we shall have perfected to parry against misfortune till age doth make the blood go slow. Then shall we be grateful following a long healthy life to

lie that final night asleep in bed, to be mourned only by
dawn's early pale light, and for it always to be known we
played De Alfonce.

## THE FUNERAL

Although fellow players will be sentimentally tempted,
nothing so inappropriate as wearing sporting apparel should
be ventured in attendance upon a player's funeral. Wreaths
you send may of course represent the emblem at a small
licensing charge. The coffin may be adorned by the De
Alfonce Tennis flag upon which may also be placed the deceased player's crossed racquets and ball. Such departed's
name shall be recorded in the De Alfonce Tennis directory
under deceased players. So as not to dwell on death we
remind here of the De Alfonce christening mug supplied at
a low nominal charge for such ceremony accorded a player's
children.

## THE DE ALFONCE BALL

This annual event is a time for sincere carefree merriment
at which regretful, revengeful, thwarted, long faced and el
loppo embittered personalities are to be eschewed.

Held at climatically agreeable times in various countries
of the world, this glamorously elite ball should be much
looked forward to by De Alfonce players, and a warm welcome always awaits any who have travelled far to attend. As
such soirees incline to convene a sophisticated and
pleasantly elegant lot who have outstandingly succeeded in
their chosen walk in life, the venue selected should be
accordingly appropriate. Sleazy second rate hotels, tatty
road houses, down at heel country clubs and make shift
collapsible tents are simply not on. Instead sprawling man-
sions, castles and stately homes with their own integral ball-
rooms and approached by long winding pebbled drives are
to be preferred. And in such gracious abodes, the most

desirous focus of all is the De Alfonce court itself, above which a crystal chandelier has been raised.

The colours purple and crimson in the form of flowers and drapery should be in abundance, nor spare the yachting motifs. It is customary to have upon prominent display photographs of the current men and women's world top ranking singles, doubles and mixed doubles players, which shall flank a larger centre positioned photograph of the Honourable Founder. Such photographs shall always be gladly supplied at a nominal charge from the headquarters of the W.D.T.A.

Throughout the evening at such appropriate times the orchestra will perform selections chosen from the manual which reflect the history of the game. Should the H.F. be present at any Ball, he will commence the hoofing with the Honourable Founder's Waltz. In the H.F.'s absence the first ranking male player will take the floor with the first ranking female player. In ethnically distinctive countries the native dance will be instead attempted by the H.F., and any loud laughter will be considered entirely inappropriate.

The evening will end with the De Alfonce Stomp. This is an antic in which the left foot is held firmly in place while the right vigorously pounds the floor to the grunting cadence normally conducted prior to matches with the Honourable Founder. This cacophony can be calculated to have an electrifying effect, even upon the most ice cold of male and female virgins present. However, an engineer should prior be consulted to survey the building in anticipation of this ritual. At all balls world wide, priority will be accorded use of W.D.T.A. approved beverages and victuals.

## Looking Ahead

The De Alfonce manual will be updated at appropriate times to keep abreast of the sport. Players are requested to

keep the W.D.T.A. informed of abuse, misuse, infringe-
ment or pirating of any of the contents of the De Alfonce
Tennis manual or its customs, traditions, trademarks, patent rights or new inventions. Players on the spot should
not hesitate to flap racquet at, play pop with and dress down
any guilty party caught in such heinous act.

The mantle of the Honourable Founder will devolve
upon his heirs and assigns, and his name be entered, at the
relevant time, upon the commemorative brass of all official
courts throughout the world with date of birth and death.


## VASECTOMY

This unfortunate ligature or curtailment in your posterity
will definitely interfere with your game. Much of the moral
strength upon which the De Alfonce player draws, eman-
ates from the invigorating risk he constantly hazards in this
procreative regard in his everyday life. However if you insist upon such severing or permanent knotting of your sper-
matic cord, it is hoped that ere long there will be established
the De Alfonce clinic offering, at a special rate, such sterility
to players. That the risk of an unsuccessful operation may
be underwritten, is a distinct possibility, should present
efforts succeed in establishing the De Alfonce Insurance
Company.


## DE ALFONCE TENNIS ADVISORY BOARD

The seven member committee convened for this purpose
shall all be players of at least three years' standing and rank
in the first one hundred of the computerized rankings in
the country in which they hold citizenship and be selected
for their ladylike or gentlemanly sensitivities and for their
genuine enthusiasm shown for the sport.

Members are paid an adequate annual fee for their services and such remuneration will be quarterly monitored to

accord with inflation and deflation. Payment will be in arrears and made in any currency equivalent, such member being at all times able to designate such place of payment, including behind the Iron Curtain or orbital space station or satellite which may now be or come into existence, provided however that a De Alfonce approved bank will always be given priority in any such payment designated choice.

Except for travel into orbit or outer space, all other reasonable travel expenses for two shall be reimbursed, first choice given to top class De Alfonce approved hotels where courts for the sport are provided for play.

Upon their satisfactory serving and observing faithfully all their duties for a minimum period of three years, such members are entitled to retire and to receive for life two thirds of their annual fee, such entitlement to devolve upon their surviving dependent mistress or spouse. The Honourable Founder shall be for his lifetime Chairman of such board and due to such extra responsibility shall for his services be remunerated in an amount adjudged dignified and be allowed extra terrestrial travel and expenses. The De Alfonce suite will be kept reserved for the H.F. at all De Alfonce approved hotels.

## The Institute of
## De Alfonce Tennis Research

Such prominent scientists, designers and inventors as may be De Alfonce players shall be invited to partake in the search and research for improved materials and designs for the bettering of the accoutrements and equipment of the game including diet and regimen. Except for special cases and such awards as are made for outstanding contributions it is expected all such work by institute members will be dedicated free of charge to the beneficial furtherance of the sport.

## FAT SHIPS

Treated in the serious financial light in which such organizers put it, this is a highly novel endeavour to entice those corpulent to proceed upon such vessels to sea, well out of the sight of land, and there in such bulkhead confines, trim from themselves by diet, exercise and therapy, their trembling slabs of fat. Upon sufficient numbers of players applying, a franchise will be licensed to such ships for the establishment aboard of De Alfonce courts, and for such passengers to adapt the exercise regimen routines of this manual.

However, there are unscrupulous operators of such schemes, and would be passengers are warned that an 'Eclair' ship tender so named after the chocolate whipped cream variety of this sweet, has been known to be brought into the near vicinity of the Fat Ship once the passengers have undergone their first three days of starvation regimen. These 'Eclair' ships not only carry freshly baked eclairs in utter endless abundance but also other rich food substances and beverage in every plethora possible, including hot dogs and sauerkraut, and for which the patrons of the Fat Ship are then charged an astonomical amount in their starved desperation.

These unedifying entrepreneurial promoters achieve their shameful ends by bringing the 'Eclair' ship windward to the Fat Ship, so that the pathetically susceptible patrons, enticed by a whiff of chocolate fragrance wafted on the sea breeze, are stampeded, clamouring to scale the gunwales to be first into the waiting row boats. Ostensibly in secrecy, the determined victims, are then rowed, at an exorbitant tariff, to where they then gorge. Once sated, they are then again overcharged for their return journey to the Fat Ship which, as they struggle to clamber aboard again, now runs the risk of listing dangerously. You are therefore advised to check with your De Alfonce approved travel agent before similarly being taken advantage of.

## THE DE ALFONCE APPROVED
## HOTEL OR INN

Aside from daily fresh sheets on the bed and your favourite flowers in a vase, the best test of a hotel which pretends to top quality, is to succeed, at two a.m., in obtaining from room service in under ten minutes a nice big dollop of ice cream, home made of fresh strawberries. This also gives an excellent indication to a De Alfonce player who regards breakfast as his or her premier meal of the day, that the full De Alfonce Manual breakfast will be delivered on the dot if ordered the evening before, or within twenty minutes, if summoned between the hours of three a.m. to twelve noon.

Such hotel or inn should have available on the premises, or easily accessible within its grounds, at least three De Alfonce courts, one of which provides for bulkhead and ceiling play. Attached to such courts should be a sauna, shower, swimming pool, dressing and resting rooms. However, a moratorium on such requirements is allowed, provided such purpose built De Alfonce courts are in the process of being erected, and the hotel's ballroom, or conference facility is made temporarily available for play. A ready supply of balls, racquets and De Alfonce wear will at all times be kept available for players to borrow or buy.

Bathrooms will be of marble, large enough in which to do the Manual's towel drying exercises and with baths a minimum of six feet six inches in length, and which can be filled with suitably hot water to a depth of two feet in under thirty seconds. A manœuvrable bright, bedside reading lamp so that players may comfortably read their Manual before retiring, is also essential. The windows and walls of bedrooms will be sound proofed and double doored to prevent the noise of staff, street traffic or another guest reaching the ears of a sleeping De Alfonce player. A chamber pot, not necessarily with the De Alfonce emblem, must be within bed reaching distance.

Bedrooms will be adequately large enough, with furnishings manœuvrable, for players to practise against at least one wall, and with mirrors enough for such practice to be self observed. 'His' and 'Hers' copies of the present Manual are to be made available in all guests' chambers. But as these are likely to accidentally disappear in the luggage of non De Alfonce players, hoteliers are advised to discreetly exhibit a reminder that an appropriate charge will be made on a guest's bill for such removal.

Under no circumstances, while a De Alfonce guest is in residence, is the smell of paint or other disagreeable fume to be allowed to flow through the hotel. Nor are pneumatic drills, sawings, thumpings, or hammerings to be done by day or night, even when they are thought incapable of breaching the sound proofing.

The usual De Alfonce discount will be accorded all De Alfonce players on presentation of their identifying De Alfonce credential. The Honourable Founder and his guest will be permitted to stay free of any charge at all De Alfonce approved hotels, and the appropriate De Alfonce flag will be flutteringly flown from the hotel's masthead while the Honourable Founder is in residence.

## Your Health Club

Before joining, you are respectfully advised to check for a De Alfonce approved establishment which will be regularly inspected not only for its courts but for De Alfonce standards. As in the American slang words of Lord Charles, some of these places can prove to be sleazy and slimy indeed. Fungus complaints between the toes especially are rampant, including more serious diseases transmitted by moist warm contact not to mention the poisonous applications commoners are prone to use for deodorizing.

If you cannot afford the higher charges of the De Alfonce approved venue then choose carefully and don't get inveigled into places where it is not possible to swing a cat. Make sure the exercise equipment is in good order before using and not likely to crush your fingers or in falling on you, break a limb. Bring your own towel and soap and wash in the hottest water you can stand. Keep at least an arm's length away from other poor patrons like yourself. Getting to know one another might make you both break down in tears. Do also look into the pool water. Although this may be entirely transparent without moulds and algae present, contrary to what you may think, this may actually mean at least something can live in the water, which proves it's not laced with an eye searing solution of chlorine, carbolic or other bactericidal agent which can cauterize your skin.

After determining that the facilities are not liable to be damaging to your health, you would be wise to consider, the not inconsiderable matter of such places, irrespective of the celebrity membership being boasted of, being devastating to your social standing.

## ATHLETE'S FOOT

A devilish old damned difficulty this, producing scaling and inflammation as the outer skin thickens, turns white, peels off, and finally painfully cracks. Trouble usually starts between the toes, causing not only continuous discomfort while out boulevarding but also just as you are trying to go to sleep at night, or contemplate other matters while next to your enamoured. However, no recent cases, that the Honourable Founder is aware of, have proved fatal. But as other parts of the body, including your racquet wielding hands, can become involved, care to control it should always be taken but avoid steps to a complete cure as these could be worse than the affliction.

Alas this mouldy mycelium may perpetually lurk on your skin or even in your best athletic and bath facilities, which is also an excellent hygienic reason why you should not borrow or steal someone else's sweaty socks nor purloin another's disreputable looking sneakers. Nor should you, unless it be De Alfonce approved, take tubes or sprays of stuff advertised to kill these several little fungal species, as such are likely to poison or gas you in the process. Also do not hesitate to shout loudly to those using such nearby, to be rapidly and distantly away from you in a hurry.

Helpful treatment, subject to your physician's approval, can take the form of wearing open toed sandals which of course, makes it awkward if, like Lord Charles, you like kicking commoners. Itching discomfort can be allayed by stingingly anointing the affected parts with alcoholic spirits, a liquid which also might help keep the fungus lying low, but alas, even upon routine systematic application, such cannot be guaranteed to get rid of this affliction, which at least, should you conspicuously suffer from it, can be taken as some sign of being an athlete.

## BATH WALLOWING

It is extremely important to remember that the shower manner of cleansing should not displace this routine of ablution. The warm enfolding suitably scented and bubbled waters give to both body and mind an especially beneficial reassurance.

## THE OLDER DE ALFONCE PLAYER

Alas, be diplomatic in handling a defeated younger player. It is highly objectionable to get up on your superior high horse by announcing your age and patronizing a player half your years who has just hopelessly sweated and fought every point into el floppo defeat, unless of course he has been a bit of a Lord Charles and flung his racquet down and kicked a dusty smudge or two on the Club's ebony net mast and cursed your white flowing locks beneath his breath. Then, by god, there is no need to lessen his ignominy.


## MERCHANDISING

With all these patent and trademark scrutinizing pirates and thieves around the globe, and assuredly also somewhere out there in the megagalactic cosmos, who are watering at the mouth ready to pounce, this alas is a most certainly necessary subject to broach.

However, to all those honest merchants among you, and who need not perhaps be reminded that they will have to secure crystal clear written permission, but who are nevertheless courteously reminded, you will also be happy to know, that you may, subject to licence and such licence giving you the right to take proceedings against any infringer without expense to the Honourable Founder, manufacture a bright blue-eyed Laura wind-up doll of exquisite beauty, which also may be festooned with equally attractive toy gems or the real thing in the de luxe version.

In the case of a blond-haired, Lord Charles wind-up speaking doll, the spring of which will have to be of heavy duty steel in order that its arms will gesticulate fully and both legs kick high when such appendages are activated, there will also have to be a powerful battery to ensure that the laugh is uproarious and that the English accent is scathingly aristocratic.

Of course microchip versions of the above dolls will be computer controlled, as will be the kit built replica of the motor yacht 'Hiyathere', which is capable of being sailed on a local park pond, or a rich De Alfonce player's personally owned lake. As to the French professor, who pretends to jump overboard from a large transatlantic liner, this may be a more difficult toy adaptation to perfect.

Merchandisers and manufacturers must secure prior De Alfonce aesthetic approval in order that such doll or any other De Alfonce accoutrement does not transgress the traditions and decorum which pervade the aesthetic elements of the De Alfonce way of life, and such standards shall apply to any and all De Alfonce artefacts.

## The De Alfonce Curse

The above is hereby declared and made known to all those whom it may concern. The Honourable Founder to whom the invocation of such curse was bequeathed, has invoked this warrant with the consequences implicit in such bane befalling those so named and proscribed. And the Honourable Founder now puts on notice all those who without licence or permission, hope to imitate, steal, misuse, abuse, aggrandize or trade upon any of the contents of this Manual, and that any who should so attempt to do, such curse is hereby and now sworn and cast upon them.

But alas to you who disbelieve, it is also made known, that not all dire threat exists in such providence alone, and, with their full seeking of damages, writs, summonses and all other legal instruments available within the laws of any nation or in any megagalactic civilization yet to be discovered, shall also be put perpetually grinding mercilessly against all who so deserve, to thereby burn their fingers and give them such woe as shall make them and their sneaky heads wag slowly in their ruin, where ere they may lurk.

## The De Alfonce Blessing

This devolves upon all true players and is here given, that they may have a long, fruitful life and that they may, in the absence of their discontent, sing of its virtues, and always rejoice in their beloved game. And in the name of Horatio, Laura, Clare and Lord Charles.

Blessed be
Our racquets
And may our
Balls bene, always bounce
Free

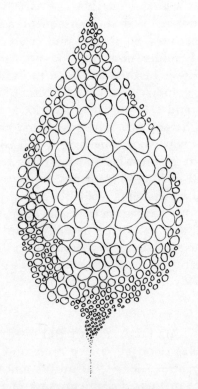

THE BUBBLE FLOWER
Discovered and collected by the 'Fourteenth'
in the darkest rain forests of Brazil, a rare plant,
the strange pollen of which gives no discomfort
to hay fever sufferers.

# GLOSSARY

ADRECTAL: The area about the rectum frequently of concern to keep in apple pie order.

AUSTIN: (taking an): With the permission of the Umpire and an opposing player or players, to excuse oneself for five minutes to disappear off court in the desperate need to vomit, eructate, expectorate, urinate or make movement of the bowel.

AUSTIN BIS: Twice the length of an Austin, and extremely irritating to the player or players who remain waiting on court.

BANGOKOK: An early version of De Alfonce Tennis, and now only played by the most ancient but still astonishingly physically fit of old fogies.

BENE: Used in De Alfonce to describe a ball which has landed in play without fault.

BIS: Twice. And the term used in counting sufficient times the ball crosses the net in volleying for serve.

BLAZE: The series of strokes in which the ball is aimed at your opponent's body area when he places himself at the net in order to volley cross court or slam a pass down the Reeperbahn.

BONNET: Used in memory of Lord Charles to refer to all head wear in De Alfonce play.

BURT (doing a); Drinking alcoholic beverage in a quantity which produces blank periods in your life, or in drinking liquids not De Alfonce approved.

CARESS: A stroke in which the ball is merely touched to anoint side spin when executing a particularly excruciating finesse at the net.

CHALURA: Term used in mixed doubles when both sides have won three points.

CHARLES: Score even in a ladies' match. Named after Lord Charles whose blatant snobberies have inadvertently played a much larger role in the writing of the De Alfonce manual than the author would have wished.

CHUFFED: To be puffed out with pleasure.

CHUKKA: The winning of four points in a game by a margin of two.

CLARE (a): The winning of five chukkas by a margin of two.

COMMODORE: The match won. Named after the mysterious Commodore who advocated punching large sharks in the nose to deter them attacking.

CULPA: Ball landed out of play or player in error.

DE ALFONCE: Pronounced Day Al Fonce. The name given the game is taken from the third Christian name of Horatio Josiah De Alfonce Adams IV. The word's original meaning: 'to display fondness' and in its use in the Old French, as 'Founce': 'to have one's attention fixed upon'. Its first usage dating from the year 1430 published in the Lydgate Chronicle, Troy VIXXXVi; 'By the power of this sorceresse I was so 'founced' upon her fayrenesse.'

EL FLOPPO: An awful dismal flop for which the perpetrator is vividly remembered and may involve a slipped scalpel in an operation or a dud offering on the stock exchange, or in describing a poor showing in a De Alfonce Championship play.

ENCEINTE: From the French, pronounced (on sant). An enclosure, chiefly of fortifications to surround closely. Or to be pregnant, as with a lady being in such state, upon which alas, this manual pretends no advices. And the term used to describe the ultimate in De Alfonce play.

EN CROISSANT: The crescent curvature of the shaft of the De Alfonce racquet represented in all De Alfonce emblems.

FLORENCE: The famed city of Italy, where it was reputed the 'Fourteenth' spent much time in his youth, visiting. And the name used in this manual to describe the area between the service court and Stern line in Enceinte De Alfonce play.

FRENCH PROFESSOR (doing a): Act of suddenly disappearing and reappearing where least expected. Named after the extremely polite French professor for whom a memorial has since been advocated by an august group of French intellectuals, to be plasced in the Pantheon in Paris.

LAURA: Score even in men's match. Little further can be said by any words which would always fail to describe the beauty in body and soul of this woman.

LAX IN YOUR TRACKS: An expression used in De Alfonce play to describe a player hopelessly caught rooted to the court as a bene ball blisters by.

LORD CHARLES (doing a): Kicking doors, smashing windows, pissing without a latrine or behaving in a purely objectionable manner.

MY CHARLES: In ladies' singles play, the score declared by the lady who is winning.

MY LAURA: In gentlemen's singles play when your opponent's score is losing.

NURT (a): Floater ball which when landing proceeds without bounce to roll along the court.

PARK WEST AND SOUTH: Boulevards bordering the centrally located park on the famed Manhattan Island of

New York City, and upon which the Honourable Founder has often had occasion to walk and cast his eyes. And the name now given to the respective end surrounds of the Enceinte De Alfonce court.

QUATER: Four times.

REEPERBAHN: Notorious boulevard in Hamburg where sightings of disappeared Bangokok players have been made.

RIPOSTE PARRY: Taken from the sport of fencing, it is the term given to rallies in De Alfonce, and are so called because of their unusually long duration, especially at the hands of skilled players and during which they crucially vie to gain advantage in their positional strategy.

SEMEL: Once.

STIRRUP CUP: A personalized pewter hour glass shaped cup with attached cover into which a player discreetly expectorates and which is kept, contents unseen at the umpire's stand.

TER: Three times.

TOURBILLON: From the French (pronounced: toor bee yon). A term used to describe, especially in doubles Enceinte play when players are in turn taking strategic shots which produce in their astonishing geometric trajectories such hilarious unpredictability, that in such whirl and bustle, players risk collapse from convulsing laughter.

VASCULUM: A case used by botantists to collect specimens and the name given to the valise used by the well heeled De Alfonce player to carry his equipment.

YOUR CHARLES: In ladies' singles play when an opponent's score is winning.

YOUR LAURA: In gentlemen's play when an opponent's score is winning.

ZEKE (a): A service which abjectly leaves receiver lax in his tracks.

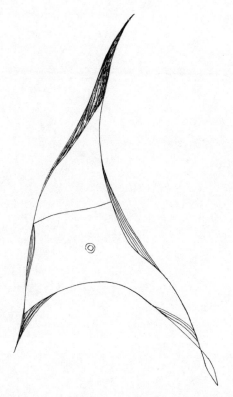

Electron microscope enlargement of cryogenically preserved
molecule of cell matter discovered by the owner of the motor
yatch 'Hiyathere', and thought to hold the secret of re-
awakening the deep frozen dead.

## Post Dedication

So as not to be ignored nor forgotten, this Manual is further dedicated to those other 'thirteen', the unsung and innocent ladies who aboard the 'Hiyathere' and together with the crew members including their captain, and numbering in all, forty two souls, vanished hither. Let us pray the gods have bestowed lenifying kindness in the awful fate rumoured to have befallen them. And may others hereby know of their involuntary contribution to the delicate sweets of De Alfonce Tennis play which they may now sadly never taste.

# Epilogue

As to the mysterious matters connected to Laura, the French professor, the Commodore and his oriental companion, they turned out to be more unbelievable than I could ever have imagined and I sometimes hysterically imagined a lot. Including perhaps the strange sighting years following his reputed death of the 'Fourteenth' or his spitting image in Florence in the Piazza Della Repubblica from whence he was seen to disappear into an entrance in the Via Strozzi around the corner. But the bizarre, and not altogether unhappy outcome cannot be treated of here and must await a decent interval before being finally made known in the further editions of this Manual.

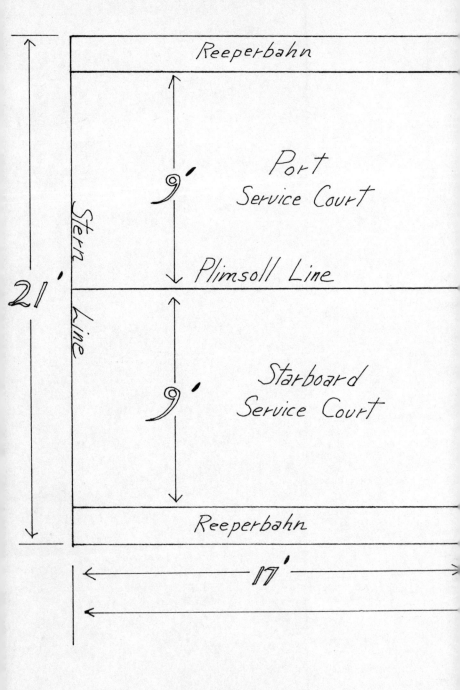